Believers

&

Doubters

Believers

&

Doubters

Why some think they can,

While others know they can't

John L. Hancock

 Liberty Lane Media

www.libertylanemedia.com

Published by LIBERTY LANE MEDIA

www.libertylanemedia.com

Copyright © 2009 by John L. Hancock

All Rights Reserved

Published in the United States by Liberty Lane Media

Book design by Kristen Garcia

ISBN 978-0-578-02304-5

PRINTED IN THE UNITED STATES OF AMERICA

Visit **www.booksurge.com** to order more books

Dedicated to the memory

Of my father

Joseph L. Hancock

(1930-2004)

<u>My Creed</u>

I do not choose to be a common man.
It is my right to be uncommon...if I can.
I seek opportunity...not security.
I do not wish to be a kept citizen,
humbled and dulled by having the state look after me.
I want to take the calculated risk;
to dream and to build,
to fail and to succeed.
I refuse to barter incentive for a dole.
I prefer the challenges of life to the guaranteed existence;
the thrill of fulfillment to the stale calm of utopia.
I will not trade freedom for beneficence
nor my dignity for a handout.
I will never cower before any master
nor bend to any threat.
It is my heritage to stand erect, proud and unafraid;
to think and act for myself,
enjoy the benefit of my creations
and to face the world boldly and say,
this I have done.

- Dean Alfange (American Statesman) 1922

Contents

Introduction		1
1.	Childhood Lessons	7
2.	It's in the Genes	20
3.	"Love" Makes all the Difference	34
4.	The Meaning of it All	47
5.	Faith of Money	61
6.	Ability, Not Security	77
7.	Become a CEO	90
8.	Real Danger of Risk	100
9.	Do not be Afraid, Be Prepared	121
10.	The Correct Education	130
11.	Non-traditional Education	145
12.	The Most Important Decision	156
13.	The Children	169
14.	Back to the Basics	186
Appendix		199

INTRODUCTION

   It has been two months since I finished the last chapter in *Believers & Doubters*. Since then I had about a dozen individuals review and critique the book. One of the most common questions I got from them was how did I gain the understanding and insight that I demonstrated in my writing. I believe that it started with what I saw during my childhood. This mainly involved my dad. He was an aerospace engineer and my earliest recollections are of him working on the space program with the goal of putting a man on the moon. Then, when I was about 7, he was laid off from his chosen profession for a period that lasted almost ten years. Rather than withdraw and lament the situation my dad took the family's life saving, about $9,000, and bought a four-plex. He went on to parlay this into a real estate portfolio that grew to several buildings totaling 72 units. To help make ends meet he painted houses, bought used refrigerators that he re-sold in Tijuana, Mexico, and was a part-time real estate agent. With the election of Ronald Reagan the aerospace industry was again thriving and at age 52 my dad was able to return to engineering. Being a key engineer on developing the space shuttle it looked as if there would be enough work to carry my dad into his sixties and retirement. But once again fate intervened. At the age of 59 he was diagnosed with cancer and was forced into early retirement.

So for the first 23 years of my life I saw my dad go from being steadily employed to being unemployed for ten years, to being employed again only to be forced into early retirement seven years later. Not being regularly employed for an extended period of time or being forced by health issues into early retirement would be considered a serious setback for most people much less having both happen within a fifteen year period. But if my dad was concerned he never showed it. During those years of unemployment he coached Little League, was on a bowling team, and took the family on several long trips. He and another laid-off engineer friend even bought a sailboat and we would go boating during the summer months.

While we did not always get what we wanted we never went without the necessities and I do not remember ever feeling underprivileged or less fortunate than others. I think this was because he never stopped believing in himself. This provided us with a sense of security that he would be able to take care of us no matter what happened. Through this experience I learned several lessons that few ever gain knowledge of. These lesson were:

1. No matter how careful you are things out of your control can destroy your best of laid plans.
2. While you may not be able to control what happens you can control how you are going to react and what you are going to do about it.
3. You are only defeated when you quit.
4. There is no such thing as job security. Always be prepared for the worst.

5. If no one will give you a job, you need to make one for yourself.
6. Never put your faith in an employer or the government.

I must take a moment to comment on the last item. For years, or even generations, people have been putting their faith, and financial well-being, into the hands of their employers. Over the last several months this faith has been shaken, or exposed as the lie it has always been. In a misguided attempt to regain security they are putting their faith in another less helpful organization: the government.

My father always warned against this. He understood that no matter how bad business and corporations are the government is worse. This is because of its coercive power. He realized that each of us has the ability to say yes or no to buying, working, or associating ourselves with a company but the government has the ability to force us to participate in their schemes. This is the reason that government will always be the biggest threat to your well being. Through its ability to tax and regulate it can control our lives in ways that even the most corrupt corporation can never do.

Of course there were also plenty of examples of people who did not handle the setbacks in their lives as well. Whether it was job loss, health issues, divorce or other personal calamity I would see people come completely undone. They would give up, stop living, turn to alcohol, or, worse, take their own lives. Often the setback was not near as difficult as what my dad faced. So this led me to wonder why some people handle things better, succeed more, and live life fuller than others?

As I pondered this question I started noticing some differences between people and that they generally fall into one of two types. I saw that they not only thought differently but also viewed the world in two very distinct ways. One was always searching externally for the solution to their problems while the other looked for it within themselves. In time I realized that this was the difference of being a BELIEVER and a DOUBTER.

So although this book took almost a year to write its beginning actually started nearly forty years ago. It also encompasses several lifetimes. By this I mean that the views I put forth in this book are based on the experiences of many others. These include those of my dad and the lessons he learned while growing up during the Great Depression. Lessons that, until the recent economic crisis, have been labeled antiquated and discarded by our more modern and progressive society. It also encompasses the observations I have made over the last decade or two assisting people with their finances. These observations were of people who were at all stages of life and range from very successful entrepreneurs living "the life" to salaried workers "getting by." From theirs and my experiences I was able to gain an understanding of different mindsets of the Believers and the Doubters. Mindsets that affect our decision-making and ultimately the life we end up living.

Nothing brings out the differences between Believers and Doubters like a crisis does and while writing this book we have slipped into a financial crisis that this country has not seen in almost eighty years. As it spread through our economy it started to threaten the financial stability of a large number of Americans. People who once put their faith into a secure job, home ownership, savings and investments soon found that faith being shaken to the core. Dealing with uncertainty many Americans are finding themselves lost and with no direction of what to do next. For some who were not equipped to handle such conditions suicide seemed the only way out; Doubters to the bitter end.

Introduction

   Very quickly I realized that the Doubter mindset that has driven these people to suicide and many others to despair is the same that limits their success in good times. Conversely I also realized that the mindset that allows Believers to succeed in good times would serve them just as well in bad times. It will allow them to weather the storm and not only rebound from any setback they may have suffered but also be better from the experience. How do I know this? Because I have seen it countless times. I have seen Believers and Doubters both pass through trial only to have the Doubter collapse under the weight while the Believer hits an ever-increasing stride.

   This book is **not** a manual on how to be successful or rich or famous. It is also not a book that will tell to you what to think or how you should think. Instead it is a book that offers an alternative and more productive way of thinking. It will help you to look at your life and question some of the conventional "wisdom" that people blindly accept as truths for no other reason than that it comes from a teacher, a professor, an expert, their parents or is just greatly accepted by the masses.

   To accomplish this the book is divided into two sections. The first half deals with where our mindsets come from. To do this we must focus on the two most influential factors of our mindset; culture and religion. This is essential since mindset plays such a vital role in our lives. You can give a surgeon the best education, the best equipment and technology but if he does not have the mindset to walk into the operating room, take the scalpel and make the necessary cuts then it will not benefit anyone. Mindset is the key! All your education, skill, ability and talent are of no use if you do not have the mindset that will allow them to be used to their fullest.

In the second half of the book we will look at several key areas in our lives and how we relate to them. These include such topics as money, success, failure, risk, education, marriage, and raising children. In a compare and contrast style you will be able to see how the views of Believers and Doubters differs on these subjects. Furthermore, through reading and exercises, you will be able to determine your own mindset, your views, and with eye opening clarity see the changes that you may be required or wish to make.

You may not always agree with what I write and that is good as long as you thought about what you have read. That is the purpose of the book; to provoke thought and for you to not believe what I say, but to believe and trust in what you say to yourself. That you begin to think on a level that you never realized was possible. Finally, that you, as a reader put it, "will never look at things in the same way again." So what you have is a book that will change how you see yourself, the world, and your place in it. A book that, I hope, will help you achieve the life you wish to have and never to settle for "just surviving" again.

CHAPTER ONE
Childhood Lessons

I am only human, I am not perfect, and your job as my son is to take what I do right and do it better and to learn from what I do wrong to avoid making the same mistakes.
                        -Joseph L. Hancock (1930-2004)

We all know the phrases. "Success is 90% attitude 10% aptitude", "Where there's a will there's a way", "Believing is achieving", and "If you believe you can you are right, if you believe you can't you are also right." These phases and others like them are used on a daily basis by employers, coaches, and motivational speakers to inspire people. They sound good and give people hope that they can change or improve their lives. After hearing them people are enthusiastic and filled with the desire to make something of themselves, to be special. On the way home their minds are full of all the possibilities and opportunities before them.

But in a few short days the euphoria goes away and most people return to the daily grind they call their life. Their self-confidence receives another blow as those possibilities and opportunities they were dreaming about a few short days before lay broken and unfulfilled. They start questioning themselves and asking, "Why can I not do what those others are doing?" Finally, self-doubt begins to replace the confidence, hopelessness overcomes hope, and the image of a winner morphs into one of a loser or failure.

The reason for the above situation is that, as good as those phrases are, believing them and benefiting from them is harder than it looks. The truth is that you must be a believer in order to receive any long-term or substantial benefits from any words of inspiration. Doubters can never wholly embrace the words and their effect will be short lived and of very little value. This is the purpose of this book. I wish to help you look into yourself to see why you think like you do and how that thinking is affecting your life.

But before we do this I need to explain what it means to be a Believer and what it means to be a Doubter. The best explanation I can give comes from the famed American sociologist David Riesman. In his groundbreaking book *The Lonely* Crowd, which was published in 1950, Riesman writes that there are two personality types in American society; the "Inner-directed" and the "Other-directed." For me Believers are the Inner-directed. This personality type dominated American society until 1940 and they are individuals who *have discovered the potential within themselves. They are self-reliant, purposeful, and able to navigate through an ever-changing world by use of an inner gyroscope. They excel in leadership, individual self-knowledge, and maximize the human potential.* While Doubters are the Other-directed people *who require assurance that they are emotionally in tune with others. They are guided primarily by their set of peers at any given moment and are willing to accommodate others to gain approval. This leaves them susceptible to the influences of others including co-workers and the mass media. They are inherently restricted in their ability to know themselves and often appear superficial.* This *existence leads to them becoming members of the "Lonely Crowd."*

With this understanding we can now look at how our personalities are formed. For all of us this started in childhood and mine was greatly influenced by my dad, who was an aerospace engineer. He was a very active investor and he made sure all of his children were properly educated, and not just in academics. My earliest recollections of this education are of my brother and me working at the apartments that my mom and dad owned. It must be understood that my dad was a type of man that everything he did, whether we liked it or not, was a family affair and we all had to be involved. So as a result they managed the apartments and we were their little assistants.

In all honesty I hated spending a weekend or summer day in those apartments. More often than not my brother and I were stuck with the work no one else wanted to do. We would pass the hours cleaning the filth the tenants left behind in the now stuffy, hot and vacant apartments and or garages. It was cleaning the garages that I feared the most. I can still recall the dread I felt as a young boy lifting and pulling discarded boxes, furniture, and other items just to have several spiders or some other creepy-crawly creature come scurrying out in an attempt to escape.

This was made worse since they seemed to see me as the source of their salvation and something to be reached at all cost. More often than not my dad would simply tell us *what* to do and leave us to figure out the *how* on our own. He would check on us from time to time, which I think was to make sure we did not run off rather than to offer aid or guidance. This forced us at a young age to figure things out for ourselves and, along with developing problem-solving skills; we gained ever-increasing confidence in our abilities and ourselves. This was our first step in becoming believers.

Of course this is not much different than any kid working on the family farm or business. It helped develop the work ethic I would need for adulthood and allowed me to be a valuable employee to some business or corporation. This ethic would even give me the confidence to take on greater responsibilities at work and make my way into management while going to university full-time. It did not, however, provide me the education and the independent spirit I would need to live life as I came to believe I could live it. For this my dad took several approaches to teach us the lessons he thought we should learn. At the time he was teaching us these lessons my young mind could not grasp what was being said. I now realize that these lessons not only stuck in my mind but also developed and shaped the reality in which I live.

The primary method was good old-fashioned storytelling. My dad would often share with me the failures and successes of people. In some cases it was people that we knew and in other cases it was the people that he had heard or read about including historical figures. He did not believe that our lives are made up of random events. He rejected the idea that somehow we were just boats in the ocean of life without a rudder and a motor going wherever the current takes us. He was a very strong believer that we create our lives and every decision we make creates our future. If someone succeeded he was very generous is his praise and gave credit where credit was due. On the other side if there was a failure no excuses were accepted and the outcomes would be analyzed and criticized in the detached way of an engineer's mind. His own decisions would be analyzed in the same methodical and calculated manner. This allowed him to be very honest with himself and us.

He would often say, "I am only human, I am not perfect, and your job as my son is to take what I do right and do it better and to learn from what I do wrong to avoid making the same mistakes."

In today's nobody-is- responsible world this would seem "mean-spirited" and would make many very uncomfortable. But it taught me several valuable lessons with the most important being that I am responsible for my life. That each and every decision I make each and every day is creating my future. That nobody - neither my boss, nor the government, nor society - is responsible for me and, now that I am a father, for my family. If I do well I deserve the credit; if I fail I also must carry that burden.

The other lesson this taught was that by critical and analytical thinking I could learn from others and duplicate their successes while avoiding their failures. I cannot tell you how valuable this lesson has been. Over the years I have developed the ability to not only enjoy hearing about the lives of others but to actually have their stories influence and impact my own development. Many times I will share with my clients experiences of others and the lessons and inspiration I have drawn from them.

Of course these stories were limited and often the lesson to be learned was not always obvious especially to the mind of a child. To supplement this my dad would often make us listen to records. Where he got these records I never knew. I only know that they were 45s of some of the most influential thinkers of the 20th century. I can still remember the booming voice from *I Dare You* encouraging me to be the best I can be, to believe in myself, and to live my life to the fullest. Then there was recorded version of the grandfather of all personal wealth books T*he Richest Man in Babylon* written by George S. Clayson in 1926 and, my dad's favorite, *Acres of*

Diamonds illustrating that success and opportunities can be found in our own backyards.

Although what was on the recordings was important, the true value of these recordings was the gift I received from my dad to have an open but critical mind. It was never enough just to listen to them. We had to dissect the message and analyze each piece. If something seemed incredible we weren't allowed to dismiss it out of hand. We were encouraged to examine it logically to see if the statement could be plausible. Even if, after several hours if not days of mulling it over, we could not conclusively accept or reject the opinion of the author the material would not be forgotten but stored in our brains until it to could be proven true or false. This process led to the habit of avoiding knee jerk reactions to new or novel ideas and that, no matter the source, they were not to be automatically rejected nor accepted without an appreciable amount of thought and analysis.

They say that the teacher will appear when the student is ready and, armed with this mindset I was ready when other "teachers" appeared my life. Initially they were more like historical figures. These included such men as the German Army veteran of World War II I met when I was 12 years old and my uncle who was a Marine on Guadalcanal. The stories of men like these filled my young mind and I was able to gain an understanding of personal courage, hardship, and sacrifice that books just cannot give.

Once I was ready my next teacher made a brief but profound appearance. While I was still in high school I worked in a store of a large nationwide drug retailer. One day we had a new assistant manager come to our store. He was in his late thirties, or maybe early forties, which was an anomaly since most assistant managers were five to 10 years younger. This man must have sensed this when I asked him how he came to this point in his life.

He stated to me in a matter of fact manner that, a short time ago, he was a millionaire but had lost it all in a nasty divorce. As a result he now has to work at the store in order to make ends meet. Like most people would be, I was torn between feeling sorry for the guy and not believing him. Of course I showed my sorrow and offered what little sympathy a teenager with limited life experience could.

Seeing my discomfort he told me not to be sorry for him. He explained to me that he had made a million once and that the first was the hardest. After that it was a relatively easy thing to do, for although they could take his money, they could not take away his knowledge and ability to make money.

A few months later this man and I were closing the store. As he was locking the door he turned to me and asked, "Do you remember what I told you when you asked me how I got here?"

"Yes" I replied, "you said that you were a millionaire but had lost your money in a divorce."

"What else did I say?" he prompted.

"That you would be one again someday."

"Well" he said while smiling broadly and jingling the store keys, "that day has come and today is my last day having to work here."

I watched as he took the keys in his hand and passed them through the metal mail slot in the glass door. A ceremonious flick of his wrist sent the keys flying through the air, spinning and turning as each one strained to break away from the ring that held them together. For about five feet they arched towards the ceiling before starting their decent on a collision course with the black and white checkered floor. The sound of the keys hitting the ground and the screeching sound of them skidding on the tile could be heard outside.

I must have had an incredulous look on my face when he returned his gaze back to me. In fact I was so stunned that nothing else was said. He just smiled and winked as he turned and strolled to his car. As I walked to my car I watched him leave the driveway and disappear.

That was the last time the man I call the millionaire manager. I never found out what happened to him afterwards and I have often wondered if he did his theatrical farewell for my benefit. I do know that he proved two of my dad's lessons:

Money is not important,
It is your ability to make money that counts
Failure does not make us failures,
It is what we do afterwards that does

Twenty plus years later as a financial advisor and tax preparer I have had the opportunity to meet with a multitude of people from all walks of life and to talk about one of the most personal aspects of their lives: their money. While not all of them are as dramatic as the one just mentioned, each had a lesson and expanded my knowledge. From those who have done well I learned what worked, and from those who have not done so well I have learned what to avoid. I also began to see why some people succeed while others do not. What emerged was the understanding that it is not the situation we were born into, our intelligence, our degrees or other so called "advantages" that determines our success. It is our attitude and the faith we have in ourselves that is most important.

Take my dad for instance. Many times people tell me that I am very fortunate to have a father who was able to teach me these lessons. They will often follow this with the observation that my father must have had advantages that allowed him to obtain the education and wisdom that most that others of his time did not get. Some offer the opinion that he must not have known what it is like to have limited options or just to focus on surviving. They assume he has no understanding of what it is to be one of the less privileged. To this and for the sake of clarity I recount my dad's story.

Exactly one year after "Black Monday", the day that marks the 1929 stock market collapse, my father, Joseph Hancock, was born in a small rural town in southern Tennessee. Of his three siblings he was the middle and the only boy. Soon after he was born the family moved to Decatur, Alabama where, although the nation as well as the world was in the midst of the great depression, my father had a very pleasant, if not happy, childhood. He would pass the days playing ball and often his father, Fleming, would join him in a friendly game of catch or one of the other sports that my dad loved. Life was good and they did well compared too many of the other families suffering the harshness of the times, but it was not to last.

In 1938 Joseph's world came crashing down. His father died of tuberculosis leaving young Joseph, then just eight, man of the family. This was literally as well as figuratively for at that time the options open to women was limited, especially in the South. Over the next several years Joseph struggled to provide for the impoverished family. Winters were always the toughest for they often did not have coal to stave off the bitter could that swept over the region.

He would often recount the story of one terribly cold winter when they had no coal and his mother was afraid that it would mean the end of them for if the cold did not kill them one of the maladies that was sure to follow would. One day, just as the cold was setting in, a truck arrived with a load of coal. His mother became very worried and started to explain to the driver that they had no money to pay for the coal. The man calmly reassured her that a kind neighbor had bought the coal for them, thus allowing them to experience another spring.

As a child my dad was immune to the preconceived ideas that limit most adults. He would come up with novel solutions for problems he was too young to completely understand. Finding a job at a time when one in every four workers was unemployed was difficult for even the most hardworking man much less a boy. To overcome this he would do what most men refused to do: he would work for free. Sometimes those he helped would pay him and on his return home he would give his mother what few cents he earned. Whether it paid or not my father always felt that the time was not wasted. Even if he did not get money he always learned something new, and for my dad time is truly wasted only if you did not learn something.

Trying to earn money during school time was always a challenge and again my father's independent thinking found a solution. At the age of twelve he obtained a job cleaning the local cinema. After the last showing he would sweep the theaters and remove all the trash. Since the last show would end after 10 p.m. it was too late to make the long journey to his home only to return to school in the morning. To overcome this difficulty he created a bunk in an unused storage closet at the cinema where he would sleep on the school nights that he worked.

This arrangement lasted for a few years but as he progressed into high school he found it more and more difficult to keep up with his studies and make the needed money by working part time. At the age of 16 he dropped out of school and went into the Navy. "The Navy was the best thing that happened to me" he would

say, "and I took full advantage of all they offered."
After boot camp he was trained as an Aircraft Structural Mechanic and soon found himself on the pacific island of Guam. The year was 1950 and, although a war was raging on the Korean peninsula, the threat to his life came from the few Japanese leftovers that continued to fight a war that ended five years earlier.

  At that time Guam had very little to offer in way of entertainment so my father studied and earned his high school diploma. After his four-year enlistment was up he earned a drafting degree from the local community college while working nights at Los Angeles International airport. With this he started his illustrious career in the aerospace industry which would include him working on some of our nations top projects including the Apollo program, B-1 bomber, and finally being capped off as a key engineer for the Space Shuttle program.

  Anyone who works in the aerospace industry knows that employment can be anything but stable. One would work just as long as the contract for the project lasted and then be out of work. I can still recall my dad making phone calls to his engineer buddies to see if they needed engineers where they were working. In most cases it would only last a week or two but the end of the Vietnam War and the termination of the space program marked an employment drought that would last for several years. While most men would despair over such a hiatus my dad did what he had done since he was a young boy: he rolled up his shirtsleeves and dedicated himself to providing for his family and, just as when he was a young boy, he came up with unique solutions without limitations.

  My dad put some of the skills he developed in his childhood to use and, with a fellow engineer, started painting houses. At the same time he took all the money is his retirement and, to the disbelief of many, purchased his first rental property effectively leaving us without any reserves. By the time Reagan became president and my dad was able to return to engineering he was owner of over 70 units, thus ensuring he and my mother a comfortable leisurely life when he retired at age 59.

Yes my dad had opportunities that many did not have then and most do not have now. As a young boy he had opportunities that challenged and developed his courage and confidence. This courage and confidence allowed him to step into a man's shoes and fill them to their fullest. The courage and confidence to resist the limitations that weaker people tried to impose on him. The courage and confidence not to follow the pack like animals to the slaughterhouse and to believe he can do something different with his life.

All of the above gives me a unique perspective on what it takes to be a believer. I have read many books on this subject and although they inspire they cannot erase the nagging doubt that makes us ask, "can this be for real or is it just a gimmick?" Or as a cashier at a bookstore said cynically, "they (the authors) are getting rich by fooling others into thinking they can be rich." My dad taught me to have faith in myself and to believe that the opportunities this country offers are real. To have faith in our system, which allows anyone, regardless of their gender, race, nationality, and starting point in life to reach their dreams.

The book is divided into two basic sections with the next three chapters examining where our attitudes come from and how they influence our thinking. The second section is designed to help you understand the difference between how believers and doubters view crucial aspects of their lives and, I hope, to will get you thinking about some of your own views. The last chapters are bonus chapters that focus on the importance of our relationships and our family.

   I hope that the pages that follow will inspire you and provide the same seeds of wisdom and insight that my dad and all my other "teachers" gave me. It is my desire to dispel the lie that you need to grow up and lose the natural instinct we all have as children to dream and believe, to learn and discover. Most importantly, that you will see that by looking deep inside and questioning some of the "truths" you were brought up with you can stop being a doubter and start being a believer.

CHAPTER TWO
It's in the Genes (Kind of)

The proper time to influence the character of a child is about a hundred years before he is born
              -William Ralph Inge (1913-1973)

   Over the next few chapters I wish to take you on a journey that analyzes where our attitudes come from and how they influence and shape how we think and react to various situations and ideas.   This is a journey that very few have ever been asked to do and still fewer have taken. It will require you to look at yourself, your family values, your education, and even your religion in a truthful and unemotional manner. It is not a politically correct journey and may make you uncomfortable, but for those who are stout enough to look inside with objective unbiased eyes it will be one of the most important journeys of your life.
   Even though this chapter deals with our attitudes towards life in general, our attitudes about money are the best indicator of whether we are believers and doubters. I was introduced to the exercise below while working as an advisor for one of New York's largest financial institutions and have used it, or variations of it, hundreds of times over the last eight years. It is used to trigger emotional responses from prospective clients, which

allows me to understand the emotional connection or attitude that an individual has with money. Over time, as I became more familiar with the details of my clients' lives, I started to see a relationship between the client's responses and their attitudes in general. I soon realized that this exercise is helpful in determining a person's personality and will help you get a better understanding of your attitude.

Please take a few minutes and provide three distinct responses to the following question. Try to look deep inside and respond as clearly and concise as possible.

What does money mean to me?

1._____

—

2._____

—

3._____

—

Now prioritize the answers and circle the one that is most important. Finally, mark this page. We will return to it later.

As I stated at the beginning of the chapter we are going to examine the thoughts, opinions, ideas and convictions that make up our individual philosophies of life and the first step is to get an understanding of how did each of us gained or reached that philosophy. Is it taught or is there some sort of built in instinct?

In some ways it is like instinct in that it is passed down from generation to generation. It has crossed oceans, international borders, and genders. But unlike instinct it is learned and not something with which we are genetically preprogrammed. It is actually more like a thumbprint, a thumbprint from our ancestors that goes back hundreds and hundreds years. Our personal philosophy about life, like all family traditions that each of us have was given to us from our parents who received it from their parents, who received it from their parents, and so on and so on.

Even though it is communicated verbally it is the non-verbal communication that has its greatest effect. Any parent knows that it is the unspoken that has the most influence and that a parent must pretend that a child is all eyes and no ears. Our reactions to things become imprinted on their psyche and become a part of them. No matter what we say it is our actions that count and that is the legacy we leave them. I am reminded of a client who was a young woman of 21. Whenever things became difficult she suffered from anxiety attacks so severe that she sometimes needed to be hospitalized. Curious, I asked her how long she had suffered from this condition. Her reply was that as long as she remembers she suffered from these harmless yet frightening attacks. She then joked that she is not alone in that both her mother and grandmother suffered from the same condition. This was not a surprise since anxiety attacks are physical responses to emotional stresses in our lives and this was the legacy that each mother passed to her daughter.

Of course attitudes get modified and adjusted as each generation marries, incorporates their spouse's philosophy into theirs, and modernizes the philosophy in order to meet the demands of an ever-changing world. But it should be understood that the core beliefs that control, motivate, and define us would be recognizable to our great-great-great grand parents.

An example of this would be the influence of Lorena on my family's Christmas traditions. One of the biggest traditions on my side of the family is that we have a potluck when we all get together for Christmas dinner. The traditional turkey or ham would be present along with all the trimmings. Lorena, who is from Mexico, started bringing tamales to the dinner. Her tamales became an instant success and one of my family's Christmas favorites.

They are so popular that no matter how many she makes it is never enough. As soon as they are put on the table they are swarmed on and to reach in to get one, I imagine, would be like trying to grab a piece of steak surrounded by a pack of starving pit bulls. If you're lucky enough to get one you need to count your fingers to make sure you still have them all. While my family has adopted a traditional Mexican Christmas custom it has not changed its beliefs. The beliefs we hold are still fundamentally the same as those of our grandparents and great grandparents.

To understand this process you must imagine your mind as a hard drive on a computer with all your memories being stored and accessed both consciously and subconsciously. It is said that people are the sum of their experiences but I believe we are more than that. The attitudes, behaviors, values, and customs modeled to us by our parents also find their way onto our internal hard drive just like those of their parents got on theirs and so forth back generation to generation. This is why we often find ourselves almost instinctively sounding or acting like our parents. And whom do you think they sound like?

Similar to a hard drive you can delete individual files in your mind and replace the old data with new. This is how we have progressed and what was acceptable, such as slavery, is now unacceptable. But this can only happen if we remove the old data and replace it with a new file. This is where the silence has its greatest effect. For most of us on many important aspects of our lives there is no new data and, without knowing it, we default to the old. If there is new data it is often faulty since it is more likely derived from pop culture and what is commonly called "conventional wisdom".

> The chains of habit are too weak to be felt until they are too strong to be broken.
> - Samuel Johnson (1709-1784)

Of course like a hard drive a little bit of data from the deleted files remain, almost like a thumbprint, in our psyche. This data can influence our thinking and how we react emotionally to the given situation. Some data is so deeply ingrained that it is never completely removed. This is especially true in the case of societal norms and religious beliefs that, no matter how hard we try avoiding them, continue to influence the conduct of families for generations.

"There are two primary choices in life: to accept conditions as they exist, or accept the responsibility for changing them."
—Denis Waitley (1933-   )

Since societal norms are so ingrained in our psyche we need to gain a more in-depth understanding of the structure of various societies and how they continue to influence us. The evolutionary philosopher Henri Bergson was the first to define societies in his 1932 book titled *The Two Sources of Morality and Religion*. He described two basic societal structures in the world, the Open Society and the Closed Society. The completely Closed Society and the completely Open Society are at the extreme ends of a spectrum with all societies, from the tribal to the national level, assuming a form that is in between.

Closed	Society	Open
Traditional		Liberal
Group Focused		Individual Focused

    To help understand a closed society Bergson offers the beehive as an illustration. Each bee has its place and role within the colony and does nothing, except in movies, to change the established order. This analogy seems to confirm French political thinker and historian Alexis de Tocqueville's (1805-1859) opinion that the powers that control the closed society "covers the surface of [the] society with a network of small complicated rules, minute and uniform, through which the most original minds and the most energetic characters cannot penetrate to rise above the crowd."

    American sociologist David Riesman went even further when he stated that all societies of the world belong to one of three cultures.

Traditional-Directed Culture

This culture develops in societies with high birth rates and high death rates, which means that the growth rate of the population is near zero. In these societies the children are raised to replace their parents. So the education of the child is focused on teaching him to do what the father is doing. Thus the child of a baker is expected to become a baker and will be taught the skills to do so. Today there are very few examples of Traditional-Directed cultures and it has very little significance in most western societies.

The Inner-Directed Culture

This culture develops in societies experiencing large expansion due to high birth rates and low death rates. It has been, until recently, the dominant culture of western civilization since the Renaissance (1300s) and was instrumental in the biggest leap of human achievement that the world has ever seen. In these societies children are no longer destined to follow in their parents' footsteps as the demand of the growing population creates ever-increasing opportunities. In this case the future of the children cannot be assumed. This unknown requires the education of the children to focus on principles that will serve them well regardless of the path they choose. Schooling focuses on the basics of reading, writing, and arithmetic since these give the individual the skills needed to learn, express oneself, and to problem solve.

The Other-Directed Culture

This is a relatively new culture type that came into dominance around 1940. This comes from cultures that return to an almost zero population growth rate by having low birth and death rates. At the foundation of this society type is the assumption that opportunities are limited and that most children will end up working in a bureaucratic organization such as the government or a corporation. The society, including parents and educators, prepares its children to take their rightful place within the organizations. This means that conformity, sensitivity, and thinking "correctly" become the focus of the children's development.

From these descriptions it is clear that both the Traditional and Other-Directed cultures are subsets of the closed society since the future of the individual is assumed. This creates a sense that individuals lack control over their lives and it drives them to seek security within the group by conforming to the norms or customs of the society. The famed economist F.A. Hayak discovered that this culture leads to a situation where "the beliefs of the great majority of what was right and proper were allowed to bar the way of the individual innovator." The group provides a level of security and comfort that the individual cannot achieve alone. The individual will sacrifice him or herself for the good of the group and the loss of personal freedoms and individualism is the cost of this security. It functions on the belief that a select elite at the top knows best. The customs and norms of the society radiate from this group down through the masses and create the established accepted order. This is man's vane attempt at trying control his environment and the resultant society is of human design. Acceptance by the group is of paramount importance and as a result individualism and individual thought is discouraged by the society since it can upset the established system.

> He who does anything because it is the custom, makes no choice.
> - John Stuart Mills (1806-1873)

The Open/Inner-Directed Society, by contrast, is based on the theory of Spontaneous Order. This theory, which was first articulated by the Dutch-born but British educated political philosopher and economist Bernard de Mandeville in 1714, praises the virtues of individualism and recognizes that there are Natural Laws that control human behavior. At its core, according to Dr. Frederick Hayak (1899-1992), is the belief that human knowledge and wisdom is so vast and infinite that it cannot exist in one person or group of people; that the only way to take full advantage of this knowledge is to entrust every individual within the society the freedom to use his piece of the knowledge for personal as well as societal prosperity. The society is thus designed by human action not by human design.

In other words it recognizes that a culture is made up of individuals and if allowed to bloom the culture will bloom also. The rules and norms of that society are structured so that the innovative and creative individual can thrive. The laws protect the individual, his freedoms, and his rights. The core value is that the more individuals who prosper the more the society as a whole will prosper. Those who learn to adapt, overcome, and improvise will be richly rewarded. Of course this calls on all individuals to do the most with the abilities they have, and those who choose not to may find themselves facing "unfair" hardships.

The main advantage of the Open society is that there is social mobility where an individual through his own efforts can leave the drudgery of the lower class and obtain some level of comfort. The Closed society limits the individual's ability to alter his lot in life and sentences him to a life determined by his birth.

This cultural lesson is more than an academic exercise. As I stated above, little bits of information or data stay in an individual's psyche and are passed on from generation to generation through verbal and nonverbal communication. This data is not always passive and will often exert influence on our thinking and emotions.

It's in the Genes (Kind of)

When this happens it usually takes the form of an inspiration or intuition. If we are not aware of these influences then the values, beliefs, and customs of our ancestors may be subconsciously directing our decision-making and emotional responses.

This can affect all aspects of our lives and we often see its effects in the public arena. An excellent example is the debate that has raged for the last 20 or 30 years over bilingual education. I believe most parents want their children to have as many advantages in life as possible and this includes learning the language that will be most beneficial to them in the society in which they live. As a result I cannot understand why any responsible parents would want their children to focus their attention on what is a secondary language in the United States. Yet this debate has created a movement led by multi-culturalists, minority activists, educators, and politicians, many of whom are third or fourth generation Americans.

A few years back, while listening to talk radio, I heard a caller telling the host why it was important for his children to learn Spanish, which was the caller's native language. The gist of the conversation went like this:

Radio host: The fact is that English is the de facto language of the United States, all business is done in English, and not to be proficient in the language of the country in which you live in is a severe handicap.

Caller: While that is true it is more important that my children know their culture and their heritage.

Radio host: So it doesn't matter that the only job your kids will be able to find is cleaning other people's toilets.

Caller: If that is what they want to do it is okay with me.

Radio host: Well I guess that your kids will be cleaning my kids' toilets.

Caller: If that's the way it has to be for my kids to keep their heritage and culture so be it.

Radio host: Well I guess I just want more for your children than you do and that's pretty sad.

   With a degree in International Business I know the importance of speaking multiple languages. It has always been a goal of mine to have the ability to communicate in several languages and I am fluent in two (English and Spanish) and have a basic understanding of two more (Brazilian Portuguese and Italian). While my children are bilingual it would not have been so if we had to sacrifice their proficiency in the language of the society in which they live and upon which their futures depends. So I could not understand how the caller could think that way until I started to understand the differences between a closed and open society. Looking back it is now clear to me that the radio host and the caller were representative of these two societies. The radio host obviously represented the Open society with its emphasis on success while the caller's emphasis on tradition, culture, and heritage, represented the Closed society.

   Once we understand this we can see why movements, such as bilingualism and multiculturalism, have such a large following including some very educated and intelligent people. It must be remembered that many of these people's grandparents and great-grandparents came from traditionalist cultures that emphasized the comfort and security provided by the group. It is also not by accident that Hispanic race-based groups like MeCha uses mottos such as- *Por La Raza todo. Fuera de La Raza nada* (Everything for the race, nothing out of the race. It appeals to the need of its members to belong to and seek security within a group. This is why it is more important that their children retain their culture and remain part of the group. They would rather disadvantage their children rather than have them leave the group in order to prosper. Of course, foreign-language speakers are not the only group in which we see the effects of the Closed society. Many sub-cultures long established within the United States seek to control its members with use of such terms as sellout, traitor, race traitor, or Uncle Tom.

> Everything for the Race- Nothing out of the race
> — Motto of the Ethnocentric Hispanic group MeCha

Even in the world of politics we see a battle between Open and Closed societies being waged as the idea of political correctness gains popularity. This idea threatens our very existence and the thought that there is one correct way of political thinking rings of totalitarianism and should be abhorrent to anyone who cherishes freedom. It should be remembered that political correctness is just a fancy label for group think, and it might be good to remember what was politically correct in regards to the Jews in Nazi Germany.

Please understand that I am not saying that one way is right and the other way is wrong, but since you are reading this book I must assume that you are interested in the differences between believers and doubters and what makes them that way. Having faith and believing in one's self is individualistic in nature and a side-by-side comparison shows that a Closed society mentality (CSM) is not conducive to such a lifestyle.

Society Type	
Closed	Open
Seeks Security	Seeks Personal Freedom
Conformist	Non-conformist
Risk Adverse	Willing to Take Risk
Low Personal Responsibility	Personal Responsibility
Resistant to Change	Change is Good
Relies on Group	Rewards Individual Initiative
Discourages Individual Thinking	Encourages Individual Thinking

As you will discover in later chapters seeking security in conformity is an anathema to being a Believer. The fear created by self-doubt leads to us to seek security by conforming to the standards of the group and results in us living life by the terms others set for us. This lack of personal faith and the desire to conform drives us to continually compare ourselves to others in our social group and to continually maintain their approval.

It's in the Genes (Kind of)

A Note on Culture

There are very few things that are as personal as culture and religion (see next chapter) and I wish to address some of the issues that arise when one tries to discuss these topics. Let me make myself clear: culture is not racial. I say this because, to my surprise, I get called a racist because of the views I hold. The mindsets of the Believers and the Doubters are found in all racial groups. Anyone, regardless of the color of their skin, is capable of becoming a Believer by changing how he thinks. In this manner I am truly living Dr. Martin Luther King's plea to judge not by "the color of their skin but by the content of their character." In this sense I am a culturalist. I detest any culture that preaches fear, helplessness, and hopelessness to keep its members down. I abhor any culture that elevates its lowest criminal elements while destroying its real heroes. This is a culture going nowhere but down.

With that said, no culture or religion is perfect. They all have some aspect or potential to surpress the human spirit that calls on us to be the best we can be. Whether by God or nature we were all given a brain that has the ability to analyze and reason. Is is your duty as a member of mankind to use these abilities to discover what is the right path for you and to take that path regardless of what anyone else says. To do otherwise is to follow blindly, the result of which is to deny yourself the one attribute that sets us apart from the animals.

CHAPTER THREE
"Love" Makes All the Difference

For the love of money is at the root of all kinds of evil
-1 Timothy 6:10 (NLT)

The 20th century philosopher Karl Popper who, during the high days of Nazism and communism, added to Bergson's thoughts on cultures by putting forth an argument on the different roles religion plays in the two societies. Popper realized that religion plays an important role and is very often the instrument that determines and communicates the norms and morals of the society. These norms and morals often influence how the individual sees himself and his place within the society and how society sees the individual. From his study of religions Popper identified two types with each playing a different role in its respective society. He called these the Static and the Dynamic religions.

Within the closed society the Static religion is used to maintain the status quo and it reinforces the established order by discouraging change. The tenet of the religion is that people are born into the position God wants them to have and to desire something different is a sin. For centuries this was what hereditary monarchies used justified their right to govern. "If God wanted you to rule," they would say, "you would have been born a noble. If you were born to a life of poverty, hardship, scarcity, struggle, and suffering then that is how God wanted it to be so you better accept it. Remember your true reward is in heaven." It suppresses the natural human tendency to improve one's lot in life and makes ambition a sin.

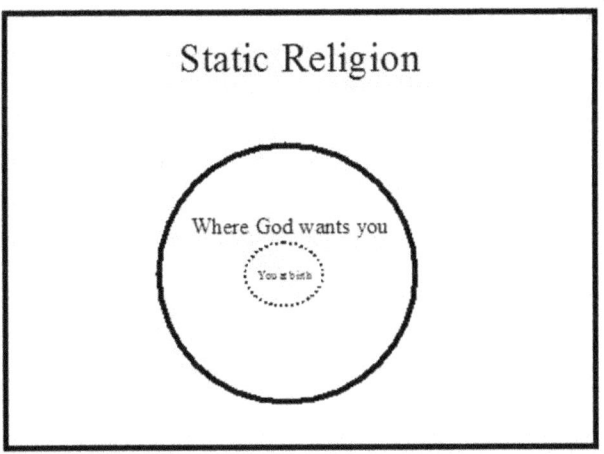

Money is taught to be the root of all evil and having it makes good people into mean and nasty monsters. To be poor is to be noble and close to God while being wealthy is an obstacle to God and goodness. Making a profit is seen as bad since it had to be made at the expense of others. Prosperity for one leads to poverty for others. This belief that change is bad and the nobility of poverty keeps us close to God caused Napoleon Bonaparte to remark "religion is excellent stuff for keeping common people quiet."

Contrary to the static religion of the Closed society the religion of the Open society inspires individual accomplishment, constant change and the desire to succeed. Hence Popper recognized this type of religion to be dynamic and that is serves its society by encouraging newer and better ways of doing things. Its main tenet is that, unlike the static religion, we are born away from where God wants us to be and we can only achieve our purpose in life through a journey of personal growth and development. This journey can, and often does, include professional, intellectual, emotional, as well as spiritual growth and often requires a lifetime of dedication. By its nature, change is encouraged and is seen as a positive and enlightening process; a process that provides us with the opportunity to grow and develop the individual talents and abilities that God has given each of us. In other words, we have all the tools we need to get the job that God wants us to do done but it is our responsibility to sharpen and hone them.

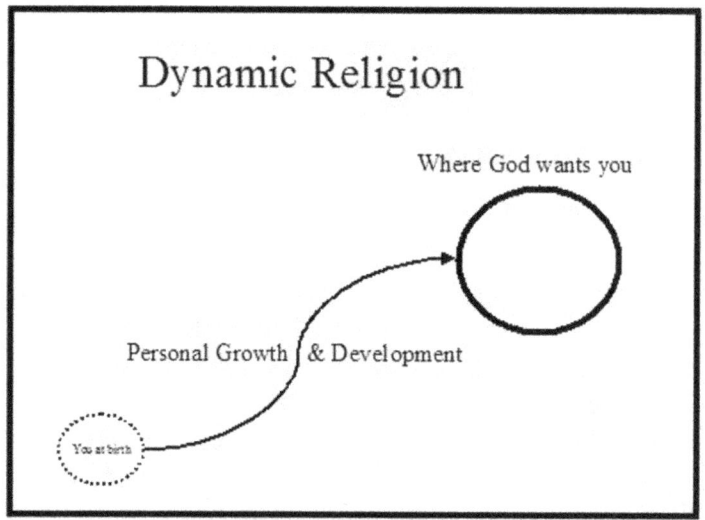

There are often several different forms that the religion takes within the culture including those who preach that there is no religion at all. This creates lively debates within the society and each group works as a counterbalance, thus preventing one school of thought from dominating the others. Wealth is not seen as ungodly or a sin but rather God's blessing for a job well done. Social mobility, impossible in closed society, is not only achievable but is expected. Society's hope is that the children will out do their parents.

While there are many versions of the static religion there are relatively few dynamic religions and most of those have their roots in Calvinism. Springing from the teaching of John Calvin, a 16th century Huguenot philosopher, Calvinism was the first to preach the principle of a "calling" in which God has a special purpose for each of us. Over time this principle, true to Open society form, changed and created the concept of blessings. The closer you came to fulfilling God's plan for you the more He blessed you and, contrarily, the further you wandered from God the more you were left on your own without His help. Whether God truly helps is not important. What is important is that believers feel that there is something wrong if they are not being successful and will search for ways to change their lives. Poverty and complacency are not accepted, and one should always strive to better oneself. If done correctly one can acquire earthly as well as heavenly rewards. In other words, poverty is the sin and positive change brings us closer to God.

The difference between the religions, especially in Christianity, is the interpretation of the often-misquoted bible verse that states, "Money is the root of all evil." The dynamic religion derives its principles from the entire verse that states that the "love of money is at the root of all kinds evil." There is a very fine but important distinction between the two. The former simplifies all wealth as being bad where as the latter has a more complex meaning. The Calvinists understood this and they focused more on how the money was acquired rather than the money itself.

To illustrate the differences I'll use two professions that both do the same activities but whose motives are completely different. The drug dealer and the pharmacist both sell and distribute narcotics to their clients and both profit from their activities. One does so to help his clients recover from or at least ease any discomfort he suffers due to a malady or illness; the other profits by slowly poisoning people by feeding their life threatening addictions. There is no way that a rational person can equate the two activities but this is what the misquotation of the above bible verse does.

John Calvin looked beyond the money by examining the motives behind the wealth. This emphasis on motive can cause those of the dynamic religion to see the same situations completely differently than those of the static religion. The stories Anna and Rachel, two girls living and growing up in the same neighborhood, will help us understand how these two religions see and react to real world situations.

From a young age Anna has had no other desire than to be a doctor. But not just any doctor, she wanted to be the best doctor she could be. Where this desire came from no one ever knew. Maybe it was seeing the doctors trying first to save and then to comfort her grandmother as cancer slowly took her life, or watching how the little girl down the street suffered from all sorts of childhood maladies. Whatever the reason all she knew is that she wanted to help people and try, if possible, to relieve them of their pain and suffering.

While growing up she studied hard and made her education a priority, often sacrificing doing the fun stuff the other kids were doing. When she did watch television and use the computer it was more common for them to be on The Learning Channel or some educational website. Being likeable and social she easily made friends but they mocked her as being "nerdy" or a "brain". As a result she had only a few close friends who understood and respected the zeal she had in fulfilling her dream.

Graduating with high honors Anna was accepted to a decent university and, applying the same dedication to her education, was, after four years, another step closer to her dream of helping people. Medical school was next and she was accepted by some of the best institutions in the country. Although it was good news, it would mean very little. Tuition to the schools was very expensive and, coming from a working class family, she had very limited financial resources. The scholarships she earned helped but were not enough and she was already thousands of dollars in-debt from the student loans she had to get to pay for her university education.

As a result Anna was forced to leave everything she knew, including the friends and family that provided the support she was accustomed to, and go to a foreign medical. Stepping out of her comfort zone and into an unfamiliar environment she overcame her fear and she dedicated herself 100% to her studies. Her schedule was demanding with lectures, labs, and then homework and time quickly flew as the weeks, months, and then the years passed. It all cumulated as Anna's parents watched with tears in their eyes when she graduated, again with honors.

A couple of years later, after a lifetime of dedication and sacrifice, and with a debt that was greater than some people's mortgages, Anna could finally be called Doctor. But that was not enough for she wanted to be the best doctor she could be. She constantly educated herself and developed her skills. She was never content to be just "good" for she knew people's lives and well-being were at stake. Soon she was getting noticed and had gained the reputation as the doctor to go to if you have a difficult situation. As her reputation grew so did her practice and medical groups were constantly offering her financial enticements to join them. No matter how good the enticement was she would never take one that limited her ability to help people.

As a direct result of Anna's success her income increased and a decade after graduating she was finally able to pay off her student loans. Seeking professional advice and guidance she began investing and in a few years developed an extensive portfolio including stocks, bonds, mutual funds and real estate. While not all her investments prospered, enough did so that her wealth continued to grow, almost automatically.

Anna never forgot the people in her family's blue-collar neighborhood and, coupled with the deep desire to help people that still burned inside her, she volunteered at clinics that offered medical care at little or no cost. While most of her patients had medical insurance and the ability to pay a few did not and often their bill would get "lost." While studying medicine out-of-the-country she was exposed to the poverty that many people of the world live in and the lack of medical care they receive. She regularly arranged trips to these areas where, along with several doctors and nurses, they gave people access to medical care they never would have had.

Rachel lived on the street behind Anna and they attended the same schools. Unlike Anna, Rachel never gave much thought to what she wanted to do in life. She was very social and as she progressed through school having fun became more important than her education, and her grades suffered. Although she did not know what a Quadratic Equation was and how to solve it she did know what her favorite stars were wearing and where she could get those fashions. She barely passed from one class to another and only with great effort from her parents and teachers did she receive her high school diploma.

Over the first couple of years after graduation Rachel majored in partying. Her nights were too occupied with nightclubs, parties, and trips to have time for school, which she dropped out of after her first semester. She worked several not very demanding jobs that provided enough income to sustain her lifestyle but little in the way of opportunities to develop any marketable skills. At the age of 22 she was an adult child still living in her parent's home and dependent on them for her basic needs.

> Modern poverty is not the poverty that was blest in the Sermon on the Mount.
> - George Bernard Shaw (1856-1950)

At this point Rachel became pregnant. The birth of her daughter awoke a sense of responsibility that she had never felt before. Life suddenly stopped being a party. To her credit, determined to provide for her daughter, she examined her options. She soon found them to be few and not very attractive. With no skills and minimal education she settled for cleaning houses since it allowed her the flexibility she wanted to have.

The static religion professes that wealth, or the acquisition of wealth, is bad and creates a barrier between God and us. *Money is the root of all evil* is its mantra and there is a fear that as we acquire wealth we become enslaved by it. Along with this is also the belief that we are all born where God wants us to be and to have ambition is undesirable since it upsets the status quo. If these are the beliefs we are brought up with then Anna, being wealthy, would be seen as someone who is not right with God and, is somehow tainted by her wealth.

Rachel would receive the benefit of the doubt since she would be seen as taking her proper place in society and accepting her lot in life. It would be assumed that she was somehow disadvantaged and is doing the best she can with the life she was given. It may also be accepted that she is the victim of a system that benefits the rich by making them richer while people like Rachel become poorer. In some ways she is seen as being noble and respected for being such a hard worker. People are sympathetic and compassionate to her situation and, if wealth is evil, she is viewed as being noble, or even saintly.

The dynamic religion sees things differently. John Calvin developed his philosophy towards wealth from studying the complete verse, which states that the *Love of money is at the root of all kinds evil.* With the addition of the word *Love* the significance of the verse completely changes. Calvin understood that money is a neutral, inanimate object and it is not the amount that one has but what is in ones heart that makes it good or evil. The determinant of righteousness is not some arbitrary amount or what people think is an acceptable amount of wealth an individual should have or not have. Instead the morality of wealth is dependent on how it is earned and the motivation behind its acquisition. In the *Institutes of the Christian Religion* (Geneva 1536) Calvin explains that:

> *we study to acquire nothing but honest and lawful gain; if we long <u>not</u> to grow rich by injustice, nor to plunder our neighbour of his goods, that our own may thereby be increased; if we hasten not to heap up wealth cruelly wrung from the blood of others; if we do not, by means lawful and unlawful, with excessive eagerness scrape together whatever may glut our avarice or meet our prodigality.*

"Love" Makes all the Difference

On the other hand, let it be our constant aim faithfully to lend our counsel and aid to all so as to assist them in retaining their property; And not only so, but let us contribute to the relief of those whom we see under the pressure of difficulties, assisting their want out of our abundance.

In Calvin's teachings we see that wealth in itself is not immoral nor prohibited by God, and can even be increased, as long as it earned in *honest and lawful gain* and is not acquired in a manner that is harmful to our neighbors. In the second paragraph he goes on further to expound that the activity that is creating the wealth should benefit your fellow man by *aim*[ing] *faithfully to lend our counsel and aid to all so as to assist them in retaining their property*. In other words, if wealth is the by-product of the desire and the action of helping your fellow man then the wealth is moral and does not hinder the relationship with God.

> Wealth is not the climax of a man's career, but an incident
> -Orison Swett Marden (1850-1924)

What is immoral is to have the desire for, or the love of, money and wealth be the primary reason for your actions. Calvin warns us not to pursue money solely to satisfy *our avarice* [greed] *or meet our prodigality* [lavish spending]. This has more significance when we understand that, just like stealing, the amount desired has no impact on the immorality of the action. To have the desire to become $1 wealthier is no less immoral than the desire for $1,000.

By taking into account what is in one's heart Calvin's teaching more truly reflects what is moral or immoral than some arbitrary number that puts a drug dealer and a pharmacist on the same level. It also brings to light all greed including that of individuals who are fully capable of doing greater good but out of laziness, fear, selfishness, and the false belief that wealth is bad focus on their own self-preservation rather than to make a contribution for the betterment of their fellow man. This focus on self-preservation usually does not leave them with the wherewithal, neither financially nor with time, to assist others who are truly less fortunate such as children (especially orphans), the disabled, and the aged.

> Don't think too much about yourself. Try to cultivate the habit of thinking of others: this will reward you.
> -Charles W. Eliot (1834-1926)

From the Calvinist and Dynamic religion viewpoint Anna, by answering her moral calling to serve and help people, is being noble, honorable, and unselfish. The wealth she acquired is the consequence of her moral actions and is her just rewards. Rachel, on the other hand, is in a position created by her own actions. She focused on her own needs and desires with little concern for the contribution she could have made to society. She pursued money for money's sake and it was a controlling factor in her life. She only became responsible after the birth of her child and then only enough to provide for their welfare.

Why the Calvinist

I need to make clear that I am not trying to convert anyone from one religion to another. I am not a Calvinist and, although I have heard of him, I was unaware of his teachings and philosophy. It was not until I started doing research for this book and I began to see the influence of religion on people that I discovered there is no better example of dynamic religion than Calvinism. While I do not agree with all of his teaching I cannot over look the impact his teachings on personal achievement and wealth have on people. The fact is that Calvinism provides an inspiration and passion for living that very few religions do.

According to Calvin it is not only okay to pursue goals it is also your duty to God to do so. It is your duty to God to discover your purpose in life and to become the best you can be. You are obligated to God to succeed! Not only that, but if you are on the right track and fulfilling the purpose that God has for you He will be there to help and support you. What an empowering and inspiring message to have to guide you. We can understand why Calvinists such as Bach, Rembrandt, Milton, Adam Smith, and Daniel Bernoulli became leaders of their fields.

Wealth, as long as it is acquired within the parameters stated above, is seen not as evil but as honorable. Calvin encouraged us to go beyond earning a daily wage. He saw it as our responsibility to provide for ourselves to the total extent our potential will allow. This included creating an estate that would provide for the family in face of any setback, including the loss of the income earner that, in his days, was catastrophic. On a grander scale we are called upon use our skills and talents to the betterment of the world. In many cases this desire leads to greater wealth that can, in turn, be used to glorify God even more by allowing the earner to provide a level of support to charities, churches, and missions that those of lesser prosperity cannot do.

For the purposes of this chapter it is not important whether you believe in God or not. What is important is that the Calvinists did and this belief empowered them to have faith and to excel in whatever endeavor they chose to pursue. Wherever the Calvinist tradition went the people and their societies prospered. The two countries that have been the most influenced by this tradition, first Great Britain and then the United States, have over the last 300 years dominated the world. It is also no accident that in the United States one in five households of Scottish ancestry, the most Calvinistic country in Europe, have a net worth of $1 million or more while their counterparts from non-Calvinist countries average 1 per 20 (French, Italian, Irish ancestry). The Calvinists are an example that, with the right mindset, faith, and believing people can influence what happens in to them and determine where they want to go on this journey called life.

CHAPTER FOUR
The Meaning of it All

*The environment you fashion out of your thoughts,
your beliefs, your ideals, your philosophy is
the only climate you will ever live in.*
— Dr. Steven Covey (1932-)

Although there are other factors that influence our behavior culture and religion affect all of us. To the extent that these factors impact our lives is different to each individual. We are the sum of all our experiences and it is this experience that determines how much the dominant mindset subconsciously influences our behavior.

Factors that alter the degrees of our mindset are the make-up of the family and the community we grew up in. The more homogenous these are the more likely we will be influenced by the dominant mindset. Likewise, if both parents are of the same mindset then you are more susceptible to that mindset's influences. On the other hand, having parents from both mindsets reduces the effect of any one dominating. This is reason the exercise in the previous chapter was designed not only to determine your mindset but also the degree.

As I mentioned in the chapter on culture little bits of information or data stays in an individual's psyche and is passed from generation to generation through verbal and nonverbal communication. This data is not always passive and will often exert influence on our thinking and emotions. If we are not aware of these influences then the values beliefs, and customs of our ancestors may be subconsciously directing our decision-making and emotional responses.

The church I attend is nondenominational and does not believe that wealth takes you away from God. It teaches that it is greed and the love of money that creates this barrier between our Maker and us. While facilitating a Crown Bible study group, which focuses on the financial teachings of the Bible, I saw how the thumbprint of static religion still influenced one of the members of our group. This member has attended the church for many years and during the study she revealed to us that she believed that to be wealthy is unchristian. It did not matter that, as we learned in the Bible study, it is the wealthy members of the congregation who build the churches, support the missions, help the less fortunate members of the congregation, and have not only the money but also the time to do God's work. To her being poor was godly and the wealthy were evil and nothing could convince her otherwise. This is more than a philosophical point of view. Her convictions are determining her position in life and, subconsciously, she will avoid becoming what is, in her mind, evil and sacrifice her financial well-being to stay close to God no matter the cost. This is how our mindset controls our thinking and behavior.

> "It is not poverty that is disgraceful but the failure to struggle against it."
> –Pericles (495-429 BC)

I have observed that these mindsets lead to two very distinct approaches to life. The Closed Society Mindset often manifest itself in the following manner:

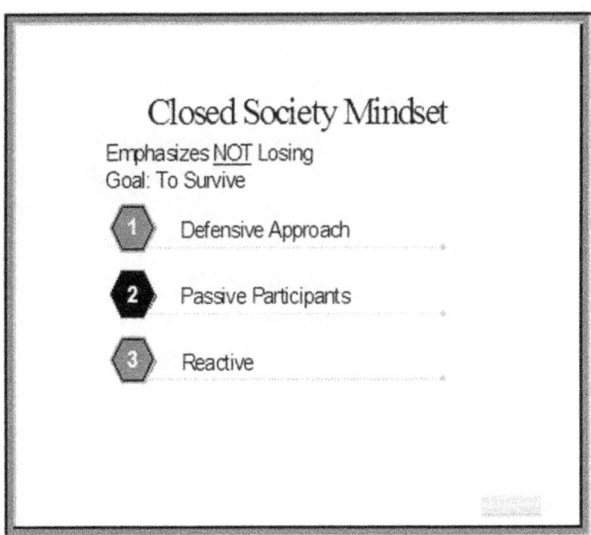

This mindset emphasizes not losing and the goal of the people influenced by this mindset is to survive life with as little stress as possible. They are controlled by doubt and fear with their greatest fear being making a mistake. This leads them to take a defensive approach to life and to be passive participants. From their point of view by not doing anything they cannot be held responsible for anything that happens in their life. The final result of this mindset is that they are forced to react to the difficult situations that arise in everyone's life. This *head in the sand* approach often leads them to be caught unawares and, like the ostrich with his butt in the air, are surprised when life bites them in the ass. Their lack of preparedness leaves them almost totally lost and helpless. In the end they see life as a struggle and I often have the impression that when they are facing the final moments of their life they will swipe the sweat off their brow and with a sigh of relief say "woo, at least that's over with."

Contrarily the Open Society Mindset has an altogether different approach as illustrated below:

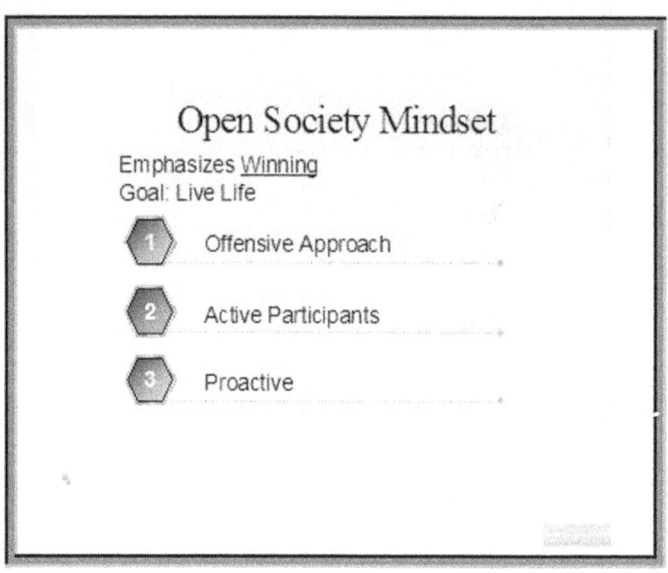

Winning is the emphasis of this Mindset and their goal is to live life to its fullest. While they are not immune to fear and doubt they are able to resist its destructive influence since their greatest fear is to have their life come to an end and not have done anything with it. This attitude drives them to take an offensive approach where they are active participants in developing, molding, and creating their lives. As a result they are proactive in what happens, and since they are always preparing themselves for the next opportunity they are very seldom caught unaware. When they are surprised they quickly regain their composure and their footing with nothing more than having suffered a slight setback to their plans. As the sun sets on the last day of their life they are likely to say, "I've done a lot in my time and I lived life as I wanted to. While most of my endeavors were successes some were failures. The important thing is that I lived. I did what I wanted to do and I made something with my life. I have no regrets."

Through my experience with asking the "what's important about money?" question I have discovered that answers tend to reflect one of the two mindsets.

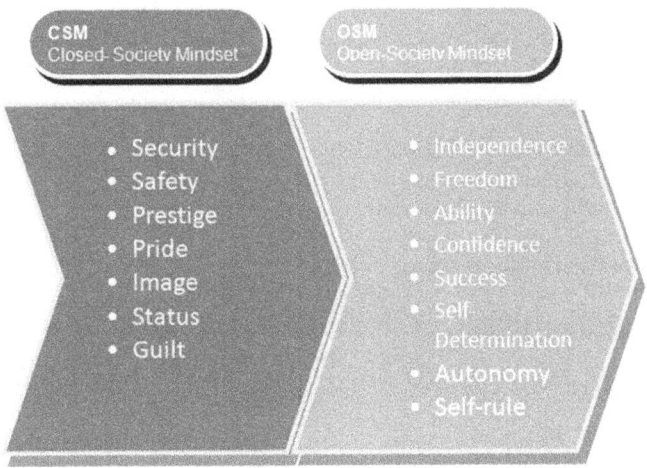

These are the motivating desires of both mindsets and are at the heart of all that we do. It is clear that these two very different lists of principles can greatly effect how one lives his or her life and is most evident in the world of politics where we see a battle between the Believers of the Open Society and the Doubters of the Closed Society being waged. One party in particular uses class envy to motivate Americans to vote for them. Even though the United States is an Open Society with its religious roots based on Calvinist Christianity there are still sufficient numbers of Doubters with tiny bits of Closed society data stuck in their psyche to make this a potentially office winning strategy. These Doubters are hoping that the village will not only raise their children but will also take care of them and they are willing to trade their personal freedom for that security. Believers, being OSMs, want the freedom and liberty to live life as they wish with as little interference from the government as possible and are willing to sacrifice their security.

Please understand that I am not saying that one way is right and the other way is wrong, but since you are reading this book I must assume that you are interested in being a Believer or at least want to understand what it means to be one. The first thing to understand is that being a Believer is individualistic in nature and requires the individual to take control and responsibility for his or her life. The Closed Society Mindset is not conducive to this and will always hamper the ability to prosper and succeed. This is why no matter how much we spread the wealth there will always be poor people. It is the poverty of their mindset not their bank accounts that makes them poor.

> ...nothing better than a flock of timid and industrial animals, of which the government is the shepherd.
> -Alexis de Tocqueville (1805-1859)

The main cause of this is the principles that guide the CSMs or Doubters. While the first two items I have listed are obvious the others are less so and I consider these items to require some explanation. These come from the CSM's desire to conform and get the approval of their peers, which provides them their sense of security. Conforming by definition is living life based on the opinions of others. The prime motivator of this damaging behavior is the fear and self-doubt that one just does not have what it takes. It penetrates our psyche and soul to the point where our decision-making abilities are compromised. It is a killer of independent thought or action and reduces the benefit of knowledge, education, and experience. Most importantly, those driven by this fear-based desire will never be able to reach their full potential or live life on their terms.

This desire to conform drives us to continually compare ourselves to others in our social group and to continually maintain their approval. This is the source of that grave affliction that affects many of us commonly called "keeping up with the Joneses." To rid yourself of this affliction you must now look inward and discover your nonconformist self to determine under what terms you want to live your life.

> Thousands upon thousands are yearly brought into a state of real poverty by their great anxiety not to be thought poor. – William Cobbett (1763-1835)

Financially it can lead us to ruin just as surely as any risky investment. In fact it is even worse than a risky investment. A risky investment is a one-time incident or event that happens in one's life but conformity, if not expunged, can affect us for life. By creating a false sense of desire conformity convinces unsuspecting individuals that they must live their lives a certain way and must have certain things in order to receive the approval of their social group. Many sacrifice their values, beliefs, and good sense in order to maintain this acceptance.

The strange thing about this affliction is that many people don't even recognize that they suffer for it. When it comes to keeping up with the Joneses it seems that everybody else has it and that we ourselves are immune to it. This is where it has its power! By not recognizing it within ourselves we can never effectively control it; it controls us. The sad part is that it makes us weak minded and susceptible to all sorts of evils including advertising.

If you doubt me just listen to advertising on the radio or watch it on TV. While the products may differ many of them have the same message.

- If you don't drive this car you will not have the respect of your neighbors and peers.
- If you don't give your kids this juice you will look like a bad mother.
- If your kids don't have a certain gadget they will be outcasts and scarred for life.

Sometimes while driving around and listening to the radio I will hear an advertisement like the ones with some snooty guy with an English accent implying that I am low class because I don't drive the type of car that will gain me acceptance and approval that comes with a luxury automobile. This also applies if I do not go to a certain restaurant, or live in a certain community.

These advertisements have become so extreme that not only are we to strive to get approval of our peers but now we need our children's approval. In one commercial a father contemplates remodeling the kitchen based on the opinion of his 12-year-old daughter. As I watch that commercial I cannot help but think that the man looks like a bloody mindless moron! I know that when I was a child my parents never came to me for financial advice or to make adult decisions for them. Why? Because they were the parents and, as such, it was their job to model good decision-making skills for me.

Unfortunately, as David Riesman points out, the type of parenting demonstrated in the commercial has now become the norm. It is the by-product of a society that has become dominated by the "Other-Directed" or Doubter personality type. The desire for "love" and approval increasingly creates "doubt as to how to bring up children." Consequentially parents "turn to other contemporaries, for advice; they also look to the mass media and, in effect, **to their children**" for guidance. This brings into being a dynamic where the children become decision-makers within the family. The end result of which is a situation in which the children are "bringing up" the parents.

There are some commercials I find very useful. One in particular helps me to assist people determine if they suffer from keeping up with the Joneses. That commercial is the one where people are walking around with their nest egg. What the egg really represents is their net worth and some of them have big ones while others have little ones. Before we can completely understand how this commercial can benefit us we need to calculate our net worth.

You do this by imagining that you took all you own (house, car, retirement plans, checking and savings accounts, everything) and sold or exchanged it for cash and then paid off everything you owe (mortgages, credit cards, automobile loans, etc.) what would you have left over? This is your net worth

Now imagine that number hung on a plaque around your neck for everybody to see. For many of you it would be a negative number letting everybody know how much in debt you are. For others it might be a small but positive figure. For a few, very few, it would be a number that one could be proud of. If this is the case, would you be driving the car you drive, or living in the house in which you live? How about dressing, getting your hair done, or the other things we do to impress? They wouldn't be very impressive anymore would they?

Owning a nice car, having a big house, or looking our best is not a bad thing. We should all strive to achieve all that we can but if "dress to impress" is the mantra you live by then you might want to reconsider things. This is especially true if you thought "no I would not live here nor drive this car if I had to show everybody how I'm doing financially" because you may be doing things for the wrong reasons. When your motivation for those things is to impress others by keeping up with the Joneses you can never have a fulfilling and satisfying life. If on the other hand you say no matter what anybody thinks I would live here in this house or I would drive this car or I am doing what I want to do then you are to a degree a Believer in yourself.

I am not a car person. For me a car is a tool or instrument to get me from point A to point B. I do love to travel and when I was 21 I sold everything I owned, which came to about $1600, and went to England for several months. I returned completely penniless and for many this may have seemed rash or unwise but for me it was an educational experience that I could not get anywhere else. It was a lifetime goal and achieving it gave me the confidence to set and pursue even grander goals. One of these goals was to return to London and this past February, after 20 years, I did just that with my 13-year-old son. It was in an adventure that neither I, nor my son, would ever forget.

This, my friends, is living life as a Believer. When you get to the point that you are so comfortable with yourself and so confident in your abilities that you do not need approval from friends, family, coworkers, or complete strangers then you are truly living life.

The good thing is that most of us do not have a 100% CSM or OSM (Open Society Mentality) but a combination of the two. Being at the extremes would make us either cautious to the point that life would not be worth living or reckless to the point of putting those same lives in extreme danger. But it cannot be 50/50. One mentality will dominate and that will be the driving force of our decision-making. To establish which mentality dominates your decision-making you need to refer back to the answers you gave to the question at the beginning of the chapter and then refer to the chart on the next page. This chart shows the most commonly given answers. Since the significance of money varies from person to person responses will also vary so your answer may not be listed. If that is the case then you need to match it as closely as possible or assign it to the side it most likely belongs.

Societal Mindset

CSM	OSM
Closed- Society Mindset	Open-Society Mindset
•Security	•Independence
•Safety	•Freedom
•Prestige	•Ability
•Pride	•Confidence
•Image	•Success
•Status	•Self-Determination
•Guilt	•Autonomy
	•Self-rule
	•Liberty

Results

The response you circled is your primary response and the other two are your secondary responses. The side that most matches your primary response is your dominant mentality. The secondary responses are used to determine degree.

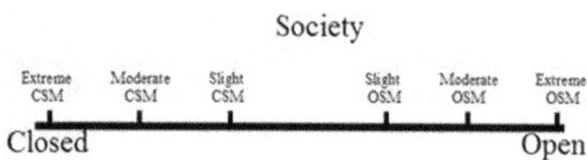

Extreme- All answers from the same side
Moderate-One secondary answer from the opposite side
Slightly- Both of the secondary answers are from the opposite side.

For example, if your primary answer is Safety and the secondary answers are Freedom and Status then you would have a Moderate CSM. If the secondary answers were Freedom and Independence then you would have a Slight CSM.

As in just about everything else in life extremes are bad and, although the question deals specifically with money, it has been my experience that it is an excellent indicator of people's life views. People in the Extreme CSM category tend to, in general, be a very doubtful and distrusting. For them everything is impossible and they lack confidence in themselves and their abilities. On the other hand, those in the Extreme OSM category tend to have an "I'll trying anything" or "anything goes" attitude that is almost reckless.

It is also good to recall that Closed Societies tend to produce Other-directed people while Open Societies produce Inner-directed individuals. The extremes in both of these categories often lead to negative results. Being an extreme CSM may lead a person to be a "people pleaser" whose opinions, thoughts, and beliefs are those of his peer group rather than his own. Equally, no man is an island. Being able to relate to others is essential and an extreme OSM person may lack the healthy dependence on others and the "people/social skills" that are required in life. In many cases both extremes lead to the same result of not having the ability to live life on your terms.

Ideally you would like to find yourself in the slightly to moderate OSM categories. Being in one of these two categories means that you have the confidence in yourself and your abilities to make educated, and sometimes frightening, decisions while maintaining enough caution to avoid making foolish and rash judgments. It also means that while you are an independent thinker you do realize that others do have something to contribute including, most importantly, their help and support. This combination will help you avoid doing nothing and hoping for the best as well as rushing boldly forward full of fool's courage.

Do not despair if you do not find yourself in the slightly or moderate OSM category. Over the next several chapters, we will continue to examine different aspects of our lives and what we can do to start changing how we live.

Believers vs. Doubters

The Believer is always part of the answer;
The Doubter is always part of the problem.

The Believer always has a program;
The Doubter always has an excuse.

The Believer says, "Lets do it!";
The Doubter says, "That is not my job."

The Believer sees an answer for every problem;
The Doubter sees a problem for every answer.

The Believer says, "It may be difficult but it is possible";
The Doubter says, "It may be possible but it is too difficult."

When a Believer makes a mistake, he says, "I was wrong";
When a Doubter makes a mistake, he says, "It wasn't my fault."

Believers say, "I must do something";
Doubters say, "Something must be done."

Believers see the gain;
Doubters see the pain.

Believers see possibilities;
Doubters see problems.

Believers see the potential;
Doubters see the past.

Believers make it happen;
Doubters let it happen.

CHAPTER FIVE
Faith of Money

> *If money is your only hope for independence, you will never have it. The only real security that a man can have in this world is a reserve of knowledge, experience and ability.*
>
> - Henry Ford (1863- 1947)

    Although quite a few will sacrifice it in order to impress others, Doubters rank financial security as one of the highest priorities in their lives. The difficulty is that most have an extremely limited understanding of what financial security is and what understanding they do have is usually gained from the media, unknowledgeable financial sales experts, and lifestyles portrayed in the movies and on television. The average person, through a combination of ignorance and lacking the will to question conventional thinking, fall prey to these images and misinformation. Knowledgeable Believers, seeking the truth, gain an understanding of what financial independence really is and who the financially independent really are.
    Even financial experts have difficulty putting a number on it and most people have only a vague idea of what financial security should look like. Secondly we, the financial experts, cannot accurately know how much money will be needed for such a lifestyle 5, 10, or 20

years from now. Many of the assumptions about retirement that were made just several years ago have proven false or inaccurate as more and more people started to retire. All one has to do is to look at the recent economic crisis and how it has thrown a glaring light on the faulty assumptions that most financial plans have been based on to see how little the experts know.

To compound this, words such as wealthy, rich, and financially independent are used as synonyms for financial security and for each other. This misconception is reinforced by the media, politicians, and less educated financial experts. On TV and in the movies a financially independent person is shown as having a large house, a luxury car, and a high income. This causes great confusion in the minds of most people and those who are susceptible to group think come to believe that only by becoming wealthy and rich can they become financially secure. Again, Believers questions this wisdom and begin to understand the truth that each of these terms has a distinct and, in some cases, unrelated meaning.

Dr. Thomas Stanley became aware of this when he set out to write *Marketing to the Wealthy.* As a professor of marketing he thought that he understood the market segments these terms describe. With that in mind he started his research by going across the country to neighborhoods that were considered rich and wealthy. In these 90210 style neighborhoods he interviewed the residents in order to get a better understanding of their financial and, specifically, their spending behavior. Through his efforts he discovered the real "OC" and learned that appearances can be deceiving.

The reality, as it became clear to Dr. Stanley, is that, while the people living in these neighborhoods had all the status symbols such as big homes and luxury automobiles, they were far from being wealthy. Most of the residents were heavily in-debt with a large percentage, if not all, of their income going into maintaining the appearance of wealth. Everything they had was purchased on credit and they owned very few of the assets that create real wealth. What was startling was that the lifestyle was just window dressing and once one peeked behind the curtain it became evident that this "wealthy" lifestyle is maintained entirely by the high incomes of the residents. More shocking was the discovery that if the income should end or could not be sustained then their carefully created facade would be stripped away and the reality of their situation exposed.

Since the rich and wealthy were not where Dr. Stanley thought they were he was forced to go looking for them. This quest led him to his second discovery, which was that the wealthy actually resided in middleclass neighborhoods and lived very normal, non-wealthy, lifestyles. The majority of them drove U.S. made cars, with Ford trucks and SUVs being the most popular, and less than 25% drove the current year's models. More importantly he discovered that they had the Believer mindset and were less concerned with impressing their peers, co-workers, and neighbors than the high-income Doubters residing in the "wealthier" parts of town.

Through his research Dr. Stanley realized that the words wealthy and rich do indeed have very different meanings. According to Stanley wealthy means having a pool of assets that allows one to sustain his or her lifestyle for a fixed number of years regardless of income from employment. As for the term "rich," he stopped using the word altogether to describe people's financial condition. Affluent is the new term and it represents individuals with "rich" lifestyles sustained by high incomes. Affluence does not indicate the wealth of the person and, since they desire to impress and are often big spenders, Dr. Stanley re-titled his book *Marketing to the Affluent*.

The other book to come from this research was titled *The Millionaire Next Door* and it became a number one best-seller. The success of this book demonstrated the lack of understanding people, including the experts such as Dr. Stanley, had and many still have. Although this book was published more than ten years ago popular culture continues the charade in movies and on television with shows like *Beverly Hills 90210* and *The OC*. With no other point of reference and being other-directed many Doubters, lacking the confidence to question conventional wisdom, fall for the myth that affluent people are wealthy and their status symbols are markers of financial success.

One of my favorite commercials is by a large mortgage lender. It starts of with a guy introducing himself as "Stanley" and he then proceeds to highlight his "successful" lifestyle. This includes his "4 bedroom home in a nice neighborhood," his "new" car, membership at the local golf club, and poolside Bar-b-ques at his home. In the end he asks, "How do I do it? I'm up to my eyeballs in debt. I can barely pay my finance charges. Can anyone help me?"

In order for any commercial to be effective it must resonate with its intended target audience and those of us with access to people's finances know that "Stanley's" situation is more realistic than most would believe. All one has to have is the will to look beyond façade to quickly learn the truth. I have always believed that a financial expert, whether he helps with investing, debt relief, or mortgages, should see his clients in their homes. This will allow the advisor to evaluate the client's situation to get a good feel for the client's needs. By doing this I have learned to quickly size up the situation and it is not very often that I am deceived by the status symbols. When I arrive at a prospect's house and I see two new cars and an RV in the driveway, motorcycles or a boat in the garage, and new furniture in the home my heart sinks for I know that the chances are that these people are "comfortably poor".

The Comfortably Poor, as I call them, are those that live comfortable lifestyles and are often the envy of their group thinking neighbors and peers who look upon them as being successful. In reality they are just as poor as those wretched souls living at the bottom of the economic ladder. They are heavily in debt and do not have a dime to spare for wealth creation. They are often one or two paychecks away from financial catastrophe and are extremely financially insecure. In fact, their situation is so fragile that even the slightest financial setback can spell ruin for the family and it has been my experience that the stress put on the family by this lifestyle often leads to divorce.

The tragic part is that these people didn't realize that they were even on the wrong track. After all, they were doing what everyone else was doing and pursuing the lifestyle that popular culture presented to them as being successful and prosperous. Did the cars, the home, and the adult toys not indicate their status and the fact that they had achieved financial success? Their neighbors thought so as would most Americans. Even Dr. Stanley, before writing his book, would have considered them wealthy and successful. This is because media, especially advertising, has conditioned us to judge the wealth and success of somebody by where they live, the clothes they wear, and the cars they drive.

As a result of a lack of confidence and independent thinking, other-directed people are driven into conformity and blindly follow popular culture. When this fails to bring the promised rewards they are forced to blame themselves. To them it is unconceivable that it was the system that let them down, not the other way around. This quickly deteriorates any remaining confidence that they have and produces the feeling that they are undeserving, unworthy, or just do not have what it takes to be successful. Unable to bear such self-criticism they often look for others on which to place the blame and a vicious cycle of blame develops which creates hostility and destroys any feelings of love and respect they had for each other. The end result is two more members for David Riesman's lonely crowd.

Fortunately I learned at a young age to avoid falling into this trap. After meeting a gentleman with a high-end luxury car I remarked that the man must be rich. My dad admonished me not to be too impressed by the cars people drive. He further went on to explain that "a car is not an indicator of how rich someone is; only how much debt they have." In his own way my father taught me to understand what Dr. Stanley discovered several years later which was that appearances can be deceiving. It was also another lesson teaching me that not questioning conventional wisdom can leave me ignorant of the truth and lead me down a path of empty promises.

In this case, unquestioningly following conventional wisdom can be catastrophic. It can create hardship and destroy families, dreams, and hope. Therefore it is essential to clarify the myth of financial security and what wealthy, rich, and financially independent truly means.

Financial Security:

Financial Security, in the conventional sense, does not exist. It is a myth. This is because to most people financial security is based on how much money one has. In this chapter, and throughout this book, I explain that money without knowledge and ability provides zero security. All one has to do is look at lottery winners to see how little security was provided by what would be considered by many to be enough money to set them up for life. The reality is that most of these "lucky" few get to experience the "good life" for a few years but then find themselves worse off financially than before they won the lottery. This is why I try not to use the term financial security. Instead I use financial independence, which I explain below.

Wealth:

Wealth is more of a measurement than an object. We will say that someone has "a wealth of knowledge" which is a way of describing his or her extensive knowledge base. Financial wealth means the same but is being used to describe the size of someone's pool of assets. The more assets, especially income producing assets, individuals have the wealthier they are. Contrary to conventional wisdom, a high income is not required to create wealth. Education and the willingness to strike out on one's own by thinking individually has more of an impact on how much wealth a person can achieve.

Most Doubters, being risk adverse, focus on saving which, while a good starting point, cannot provide financial independence. The problem with savings is that it is based on a pool of money. Like all pools, no matter how big, it can be drained. Believers understand that the only true way to achieve financial independence is to create a stream and then a river of income. Believers know that this can only be achieved by developing their abilities and talents. This is why they tend to focus on education and self-development. Only through this self-development will they be able to obtain the income generating assets that will supplement and then replace the income currently being earned by their physical labor.

Rich/Affluence:

As I stated in the previous pages Dr. Stanley found the word "rich" to be misnomer for the people of this group but I include it here for clarity. Affluence is having a lavish lifestyle that is based on one's high income. While this creates the illusion of financial security and fools most people, in reality it is a false sense of security. In any case, security, while deeply desired, is second to the opinions of others and appearances take supreme place. I find the old Texan adage very fitting for this situation: *Big hat, but no cattle.*

To understand this more clearly imagine two real estate investors. One flips houses for quick profits while the other purchases homes to rent as long term investments. The flipping of the property generates income but, unless that income is used to purchase other assets, it does not create wealth. The rental owner's properties may not be generating high income but they are creating wealth and as he adds assets to his portfolio he is becoming more and wealthy thus gaining more financial independence.

Financial Independence:

Financial independence is achieved when one has the financial resources, knowledge, experience, and ability to live indefinitely regardless of the situation. Financial Independence goes beyond financial security in that is requires ability, experience, and knowledge. In gaining financial independence one lives life with the understanding that no matter the impact of life on finances he of she can survive and even prosper. This is more of a mental and emotional state than a financial one. It is based in the comfort that even if they were to lose everything they have they know that they have the knowledge, ability, and experience to not only recover but to also prosper. These are the people who always seem to bounce back from the upsets that life often throws at us and in many cases they come out of it better, or at least stronger, than ever. In other words they become better, not bitter, by life's hardships. This is why only Believers can get to this point. There is only one way to become financially independent and that is by focusing on your ability to make money, not how much money you have.

It is very important to understand these terms because they are the guiding principle on how you relate to money and which approach you take: money or ability focused. The two are very different. The money-focused approach is usually passive, defensive and segmented whereas the ability-focused approach is active, offensive and comprehensive.

Passive Approach

This approach is just what it sounds like. The people that take this approach do so with as little thought and participation as possible. The extent of their investing is savings, a 401(k) or other retirement plan, then the home in which they reside. Their knowledge of finances and investing is very limited and they often rely on experts and, in most cases, non-expert advice. Since they have none or limited hands on experience they develop a lack of confidence in their abilities to manage their own financial affairs. As a consequence they have little control over their financial situation and when forced to make a decision it is more likely to be based on fear rather than educated logic.

With an active approach the individual strives to educate himself and gain understanding of investments, how they work, and which would be best for him or her. While these individuals get and seek advice they are the final decision-makers and accept full responsibility for the decisions. This responsibility, which frightens the passive investor, gives the active individual control over his finances and a level of confidence that the passive approach cannot give. Most often you will find individuals who take this approach to investing in real estate, businesses, and other investments that require a more direct and hands on method.

Defensive Approach

This is similar to that of the passive but with a different goal. Whereas in the passive approach people try to get by with little personal participation in the financial aspects of their lives, in the defensive approach people strive to not lose any of the money they have earned. Their game plan when situations arise is totally defensive with the cutting of expenses and reducing their lifestyle being the primary strategy. On the investment side they seek comfort in the knowledge that their money is in seemingly non-risk instruments such as saving accounts, certificates of deposits, and other investments.

At first glance the defensive approach seems prudent but in reality it only offers short-term solutions to long-term problems. For most of us a financial crisis arise when we do not have enough income to pay our bills. This may come from a loss of income or other unexpected event. For many, the cutting of expenses may seem the most logical step to take. Unfortunately this is the only step they take and that is were the problem lies since it has only limited and short-term effectiveness. It does not provide a solution if the hardship should continue and does not resolve itself or if another hardship hits and compounds the situation

If this does happen many just continue to cut- but what do you do when there is no more to cut? To me it is like a person outside during a hot day. In the morning he starts off with wearing all his clothes, but as the day gets hotter and hotter he sheds more and more of his garments until he is left with nothing but bare skin. In the end he finds himself bare and naked with no ability to protect himself. This is why many find themselves faced with financial ruin. They stayed defensive and lost the game.

Individuals who understand this know they need to consistently take an offensive approach to their finances by focusing on their abilities to make more and more money. The defensive strategy is secondary and used only as a stopgap until they improve their income situation. They are always striving to better themselves. Again, education and self-development becomes of prime importance to them. They are never content to sit back and be comfortable just because things are going well. They know that life has a way of making people pay for complacency.

They also know that they have to be willing to risk losing in order to win. Like a squirrel risks leaving the safety of its tree in order to gather its nuts for the winter these people risk their money during the good time so that they will have more for the bad. Only those who put faith in their abilities rather than in money have the confidence to do this effectively. This is the major difference between those who see their security in a pool of money and those who realize that only by willing to risk can they gain the experience and ability to gain financial independence.

Winston Churchill is a great example of this. It is often forgotten that he lost almost all his fortune in the Stock Market Crash of 1929, and while he did write several books and hundreds of articles his financial situation remained precarious from 1930 until 1940 when, at the age of 65, he became Britain's Prime Minister. During this period he was urged to "economize" or cutback, although he did make some changes he refused to give up the things he enjoyed including his annual trips, cigars and brandy. This was not done out of foolishness but out of an enlightened understanding that to remove what is enjoyable in life is to admit defeat, which demoralizes the human spirit, reduces one's confidence, and can lead to a state hopelessness. In other words, it focused on the problem and was negative. He preferred to focus on the positive and worked diligently to increase his income. This gave him something positive to do and increased his abilities to handle difficult situations. The result of which is well known.

The segment and the comprehensive approaches deal with how we view our investments. The common impulse is to view our investments, or finances, as individual items that have no relation to each other. People segment their investments by viewing all their money as being individual self-contained assets. In other words, they can see the individual trees but not the forest that those trees make. The problem with this is that investments, like everything else, do not operate in a vacuum. If our focus is on one piece of our investments then we run the risk of missing out on opportunities and at the same time increasing our risk. Each and every investment has a place and time. Each one, if properly used, can increase your net worth, lower your risk, and create flexibility in your planning.

With an understanding of these financial terms you can now develop a plan and focus your energies in the areas that makes real change in your financial situation. You can also begin changing your approach to and the relationship you have with money. You can get off the crowded paths that promise "security" but in reality lead to nowhere, and start blazing your own way to financial independence.

A Fateful Answer

It was an exciting time. I had just started as an advisor with a New York based company that was a household name in financial services and they sent me back east for training. With other fledgling financial advisors from around the country I spent the last couple of days learning, practicing, and using the "Meaning of Money" question. As a prerequisite to attend I had to compile a list of 100 names and numbers of friends, family, co-workers, associates, and anyone I could contact while I was at the training center.

I recall that on this day I had spent several hours calling and had developed a list of common answers with security being number one. It was now getting late and the offices were near empty except for those of us from the west coast where many of our contacts still had a couple hours of their workday to finish. Although I was tired and hungry I decided to wait until I could call one special contact since I knew his response would be the most interesting.

As I waited, I looked out the office window as the sun, low in the sky, still illuminated the city's famous skyline. It was not lost on me that directly across the river was one of the symbols of America's financial might and the symbol of the globalization that was then sweeping, uncontested, the world. Capitalism and the American way of life was becoming the way of the world and I was apart, albeit a minuscule part, of it all. I briefly had the thought that, since I had a degree in international business, I should visit the famous buildings while I was there, but then, just as quickly, I dismissed it with the realization that the grueling schedule allowed little time for sightseeing; maybe next time. Little did I know that fifty-one weeks later those two towers would collapse in a cloud of dust, fire, and flesh never to scrape the New York skyline again.

With a glance at the clock and some quick math I decided that it was time to make the final call for the day. My special contact should be finished with his 18-holes and be home. I picked up the receiver and dialed the number. After a couple of rings my mom answered and, after a brief conversation, I asked to speak with my dad. Several seconds past when the computerized voice of my father came on the line (he had his larynx removed several years earlier due to cancer) and said "Hello,"

"Hi Dad," I said, "I have a question for you."

"OK, what is it?" he replied.

Then I posed the well rehearsed question "What does money mean to you?"

Without a moment hesitation he replied "absolutely nothing."

At first I thought he was joking but this soon turned to disbelief as I realized he was serious. I mean, I was expecting some profound statement from a man who went from being a dirt poor fatherless southern boy with all the odds against him to being a successful aerospace engineer and real estate investor, to finally retiring to a life of travel and golf. My second thought was, since I had to review the answers with my instructor, how was I going to explain this one.

"What do you mean nothing?" I asked as I regained my senses.

"Just what I said," he replied, and then went on to explain that "money itself does not mean anything, it has no value. What matters is your ability to make money. What most people do not understand is that money is just a thing. In itself it is valueless. Its true value is in what it represents which it the worth of a given object."

"Okay" I answered in a very hesitant voice still not understanding what he was trying to say.

"Look, most people mistakenly put their faith in money, falsely believing that the more they have of it the safer or more secure they are. The problem is that money can be lost, stolen, or even confiscated by the government. If that were to happen what would these people do? The thing they put their faith in would be gone and along with it their ability to live. That is way money does not mean anything."

"On the other hand your ability to make money is yours to keep. It can never be taken away from you and as your ability increases the more real security you have because even if you were to lose everything, down to the last penny, and as long as your brain is functioning you can replace it all."

"At this point money truly has no value and no control over your life. The fear of living goes away and the only thing that becomes permanent is death."

After saying our goodbyes I sat back to contemplate what I had just heard. Although the answer was one I did not expect it was profound. It also made perfect sense and answered the question of why people struggle financially. Most put their faith in a false and weak idol.

It also made me think of several other questions such as:

- How many people have lost everything they worked for because they put their faith in the symbol rather than what it symbolized?

- How much better off would they be if they had put their faith in something that has real value, like themselves?
- How more prepared would they be for set backs if they had taken the money they were saving for a rainy day and invested it in their education and/or developing their skills?

Once again I looked out at the now darkening but still visible skyline. I noticed, to the right of the towers, a lone figure holding a light. Although I was too far to see her clearly I knew who she was and what she symbolized; Freedom. The freedom that allowed a fatherless dirt poor boy growing up during one of the greatest depression the world has seen to become so successful through self-development that money has lost all meaning and power.

Whenever it came to money my dad would always say, "it is just money; don't be afraid. Only death is permanent." In 2004 cancer returned to this enlightened man and while his mind was as functional as ever his body quickly deteriorated and the one "set back" he could not come back from came to be. Of course it made his passing easier for him knowing that his wife of almost fifty years was taken care of and that his four children, thanks to his guidance and wisdom, are completely able to take care of themselves, their families, and to live life on their terms. I cannot think of a greater legacy a father can leave his family.

CHAPTER SIX
Ability, Not Security

Deep within man dwell those slumbering powers; powers that would astonish him, that he never dreamed of possessing; forces that would revolutionize his life if aroused and put into action.
                             -Orison Swett Marden (1850-1924)

There is no other area in our lives that separate Believers and Doubters more than the subject of security, especially Job Security. Seeking Security glaringly highlights a lack of confidence and dependence on others that, while acceptable to Doubters, is unacceptable to Believers. It is obviously clear that the more one desires or seeks Job Security the more uncertain that person is in his or her ability to make a living with the skills and education they currently have. While this is also a concern for Believers they differ by striving to improve those skills, or obtaining new ones, rather than remaining stagnant and hoping someone will provide them with the lifelong means to take care of themselves. I do not see any area more indicative of our mindset than this one.

One of the benefits of being Believers, and not accepting conventional wisdom is that they develop the ability to think for themselves and gain a level of astuteness that Doubters and the followers of conventional opinion cannot understand. Believers are not willing to relinquish control of their lives and refuse to accept the job security myth. As a result they are driven to find ways to provide security for their families and this quest often lead them to discover two truths. The first is that real security comes from the assets we acquire, and the second is that of all the assets we may have, the confidence in our own abilities is the greatest and most important.

Believers also understand the following:

Whoever controls your income also controls your life.

I became the beneficiary of this knowledge and used it to create a philosophy that has prevented me from falling into the employee-employer trap that many find themselves in and, while it may not always appear to be so, to create an ever increasing level of income security.

From my earliest days in the workforce I recognized the relationship between the employer and employee as nothing more than one of convenience. As long as it was beneficial to both parties then everything was fine but if one side should no longer benefit from the agreement then the arrangement could be terminated. There was no expectation of permanency and no matter how good it may sound I did not believe that I was a member of a family. You cannot fire someone from your family. I was glad when the term "Associate" came into the business vernacular for I believe it to be a more accurate term since it does not imply a deep commitment.

The relationship is also a business and financial agreement. At the beginning, when I had limited skills and abilities, I sold my time to my employer for x number of dollars per hour. I agreed to arrive at a certain time and perform specific work for a specified number of hours. In return my employer was required to give me a paycheck each week. That was the expectation I had from them and what they got from me. I did not feel beholden to my employer and was consistently looking for other opportunities.

Although pay increases at fixed intervals were appreciated I felt more comfortable when increases in pay were accompanied by increased responsibility. This reflected my desire to always better myself and that my income reflect my abilities. This proactive approach allowed me to feel secure not only in my job but also in the financial aspects of my life in general. As long as my pay was commensurate with my education, skills, and abilities I had the security of knowing that if something should happen in my current job I could find employment without a substantial reduction in income.

I was fortunate that just as I was entering the workforce my dad was becoming a job shop engineer, which is an engineer hired on a contract basis and only for the duration of the contract. From his example I learned that you could be an employee and still have independence. The key to this independence is that you have to take responsibility for all aspects of your life. This responsibility is what scares most people especially those with a high Closed Society Mentality. It is easier for them to blame the circumstances of their lives rather than take control and be responsible for what happens in that life. The problem is that this attractive approach to life, although may appear less stressful, very seldom is. To me there is nothing less stressful about putting the fate and security of your family in the hands of others where you have limited, if any, say or control over what may happen.

When you take responsibility for your life you will begin to understand and see things differently than those who prefer to fool themselves into believing that they are taken care of. The first thing you realize is that your security comes from within and that, in order to have a secure income, you will need to constantly develop your skills and abilities. No longer will you be content to sit back and watch TV while opportunities pass you by. You will begin to see these opportunities for what they are and start taking advantage of them. In fact the opportunities to grow and learn will become more important than money when considering an employment opportunity. As my dad used to tell me, "a job that pays $10 an hour that teaches you something is better than a job that pays $20 an hour and teaches you nothing."

Incredibly, over the years, I have seen more people walk away from opportunities to grow and develop than I have seen people take advantage of these opportunities. I don't know how many times I've watched people turn their backs on an opportunity because they do not want the responsibility or may feel that they are not going to be compensated enough. What they are really saying is that as Doubters they lack the confidence and do not have faith in their ability to handle the demands of the new position. As Doubters they lack the vision to see that the growth and development is in itself compensation. The danger of this mindset becomes particularly important when the very real danger of job loss occurs and they are forced to be re-active because they were not pro-active by taking the opportunities to develop themselves. These skills, abilities, and education may make the difference between

> Too many people are thinking of security instead of opportunity. They seem more afraid of life than of death. - James F. Byrnes (1879-1972)

being employed or not and will definitely makes a difference in the income you will receive.

For the Believer who takes a pro-active approach a transformation begins to take place. Peter was an example of this process. He is an average guy from a lower middle-class family. His dad worked the same blue-collar job all his life and had settled into a comfortable but sedate retirement. As Peter traveled his own life's journey he started to notice people who seemed to have more going. Who expected more from life than a paycheck, gold watch, and a fixed income. At first it was barely noticeable but as he started to study these people be began to perceive a difference in himself. By following their examples he soon find that he had the confidence and security to take on bigger and better challenges. Fear, especially of losing his job, loosened its grip and he began to take greater control of and responsibility for his life. He no longer felt forced to sacrifice the things he loved, such as his family, or his principles for the sake of having a job. Job security mattered even less as he found himself being drawn into a profession that provided more than a paycheck.

Peter enjoyed his work and decided not to become self-employed, but he did start to look at his employment in a very different way. He no longer felt connected or obligated to his employer. He began to see his employment for what it is, a business agreement, and developed his own version of being a job shop engineer with one eye always open for any other opportunities. When he found one he was not afraid to go after it. His trust in his own abilities, coupled with the desire for self-improvement, tended to make him more successful, more satisfied, more prosperous, and happier than his peers whose fears and doubt forced them to stay put with the hope that longevity will provide the security they crave.

Even the crowd Peter associated with changed as he went through the growth process. The self-empowerment he began to feel, along with the world of opportunities he soon discovered, created a fissure between him and the Doubters he used to associate with. This fissure increased as he realized how much control he had over his life. This became especially obvious one he broke the hold that fear had over him, a hold that confined him to a life of substandard living. He could no longer relate to those who remained Doubters and, still controlled by their fear, thought themselves to be unable or incapable of influencing the outcomes of their lives.

Although it may appear so, Peter was not alone on his journey. Some of his more open minded friends, family, and co-workers became inspired by him and started their own journeys. Before long Believers, matured in their growth, soon began to appear. These positive minded individuals brought more to the relationship than the individuals Peter was used to being with. While his former friends, family, and acquaintances were great to work with, watch the ballgame with, or even to cry in his beer with they did not inspire, teach, and support Peter in a way his new friends did. Many of them introduced him to even deeper more advanced thinking while guiding him to avoid the mistakes they have made. This accelerated Peter's learning and his growth advanced by leaps and bounds.

Peter could not help but compare the differences between the two groups. In his old group he began to see negative individuals so full of doubt and fear, so unwilling to take responsibility for the outcome of their lives that they are practically helpless. In the new group upbeat dynamic people who were making the most out of the limited time they have on this planet surrounded him. He soon realized how much the others had held him back. Often criticizing him, even laughing at him, for

Ability, Not Security

trying to improve himself. While the new group motivated him to be the best he can be. His old "friends" actually reveled when he stumbled on his journey and called him foolish to think that he could change who he was. Contrarily his new friends rallied to his side reassuring him that this was a natural part of the growth process. They shared stories of their failures and how, while these setbacks can be trying, they are not catastrophic, nor permanent, unless he made them so by quitting.

> Keep away from people who try to belittle your ambitions. Small people always do that, but the really great make you feel that you, too, can become great.
> - Mark Twain (1835-1910)

As a product of the society Peter grew up in he believed in the propaganda of popular culture that claimed that those who have become successful and prosperous done so at the expense of the common people. Programs like *Dallas* and *Dynasty* portrayed the wealthy as manipulating evil-doers who get rich by screwing the little guy. Politicians using the divisive practices of class politics in order to get elected reinforce this prejudicial attitude. They stir up class envy and animosity by espousing such dogma as "the rich get richer as the poor get poorer" implying that the reason the average person cannot get ahead is due to some wealthy person holding him down.

At first these views tainted Peter's reaction when he was introduced to individuals who have gained financial success. He was uncomfortable and guarded. His sense of inferiority made him defensive and his mind screamed warnings that these were dangerous people. If given the chance they will take advantage and use him, which he vowed not to let happen. He longed to be with "his people" but decided to "stick it out" since he may learn something from them.

As time, and his growth, continued Peter was surprised that his fears and sense of insecurity were completely unfounded. These people, secure in who they are and what they have achieved, were the most generous he had ever met. They gave their time, shared their knowledge, and encouraged him to overcome his fear of achievement. He discovered that they were not special people anointed by God, but just regular individuals who overcame their personal demons and fears. Peter had never experienced relationships so invigorating, so empowering, and as mutually beneficial as the ones with his successful friends. He began to see the meaning to another of my dad's axioms:

Friends are either positives or negatives in your life. They either raise you up or keep you down so be careful of whom you pick to be your friend.

With the support of his new friends Peter became more and more successful. While not without its difficult times and sleepless nights it was not the impossibility he was once led to believe. In fact, once he got passed the mental limitations he had put on himself, Peter became quite comfortable with the person he had become and even started helping others on their journey.

We are all individuals and as such the path each of us takes may vary to that of Peter's but the final destination will be the same. How you proceed on your journey is not important, what is important is that you stay focused on the goal of taking full responsibility for and control of your life. You should always be asking yourself if what you are doing is making you more independent and secure or is it forcing you to be more dependent on others, who are often strangers. Are you taking control of your life or is someone else, such as your boss, pulling the strings?

For some it may require leaving a dead end job while others have to take less drastic measures. Pursuing a trade or earning a degree may be the first step that many may have to take in order to gain the needed confidence. My own journey included earning a Bachelor of Arts degree in International Business, which, with my job experience, gave me comfort that I could always find employment or a way to make earn an income.

Believers do not fall into the job security trap. They know that wherever they are, whatever they are doing, and whatever position they currently hold it is temporary. The sense of control they have over their lives, the confidence on their abilities, the self-reliance, the emphasis on self-development, and a constant vigilance for opportunities means that they are never satisfied with just "staying put". This does not mean that they need to become self-employed or even have to switch employers. Many employers provide the opportunities to grow and prosper by promoting within. But if their current employer does not offer these opportunities then Believers are perfectly comfortable finding a position with a company the does. For them this makes job security meaningless since they create it themselves.

> Don't measure yourself by what you have accomplished, but by what you should have accomplished with your ability. -John Wooden (1910-   )

Believers are often students of success and they learn that what is good today is usually not good enough tomorrow. This is the same for our income source. Just because they have a good steady income source today it does not guarantee they'll have one tomorrow. They are always be preparing themselves for the time that may come when they will need to search for a new income source. They know the best way to do this is to consistently be evaluating the needs of their potential income sources and making sure they have the ability to meet those needs. By doing this they are basing their income security on their abilities and not the good will of their employer.

This is opposite of what many people, especially Doubters, do and I was witness to the tragic consequences of their attitude. In the late 1990s I had a discussion with a former co-worker. He was considering going to back to school to get at least an Associates if not a Bachelors degree. I told him that he should but he was still not 100% convinced that it would be worth it. After all, he was making a decent living and school would be costly and require his time and effort.

"How long have you been going to school?" He finally asked me.

"Well," I replied, "I am paying my own way through so it is taking me several years to get my degree."

"See," He said, "I would have to do the same and would be just now starting."

"I understand," I responded, "but if you do not start now what will you have in several years?"

He never did go to school and several years later the company he was working for was sold. The new company did not need all those employed in his position. They let go all who did not have college educations and my friend found himself unemployed. To make matters worse as he applied to other companies he found that they all required college degrees. In the end his wife had to support the family while he was retrained for another type of employment. Unfortunately this was not enough to save their house and the last I heard of them was that they were moving to another state to start over.

Again, this is something that Believers understand and with every choice they have they ask themselves if the decision they are making is going to make them more independent or dependent. This may require them to temporarily sacrifice doing something that does not increase their independence. An example of this is when I had to choose a foreign language as part of my degree. Deep down I had always wanted to learn German but living in Southern California I realized it would not benefit me that much. Instead I chose to learn Spanish in which I am now fluent, have used extensively over the last 15 years, and puts me at the top of the list of any potential employer in the Southern California area. Please note: that increases in pay without corresponding increases in ability only makes you more dependent on your employer and decreases your independence since it provides an artificially high income level that does not correspond to what the abilities can get on the open market.

Believers also know that developing the ability to work for money can help ensure consistent and steady income only as long as they are able and willing to work. It does not, however, provide total security since a debilitating accident or illness may leave them physically unable to earn income. With age they may no longer have the energy or spirit to face the grind on a daily basis. They may lose interest in the work or it no longer offers them a challenge. More importantly, they may wake up one day to discover that they only have 20 to 30 years left and would prefer to do something more with their remaining years. The illustration above shows that as we get older our ability to work for money, first physically then mentally, declines. To offset this diminished capacity you must develop income from sources that are not dependent on your physical or mental abilities. The only department that can do this is Finance and it is the most important department you have as CEO.

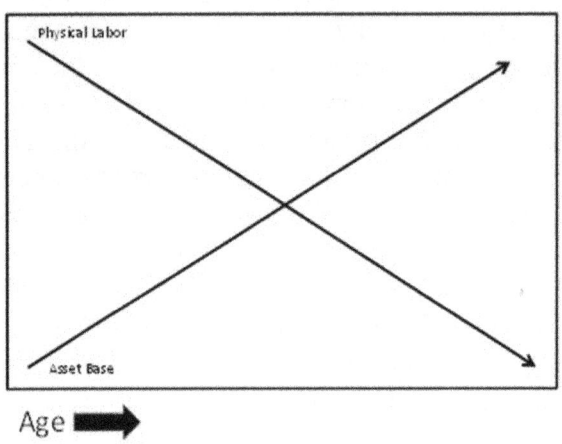

Then there is retirement. Of course working often does not always stop with retirement and I've come to a new understanding of what retirement is. What retirement really means for most people is the ability to work the job they want when they want to work it. For some it might be opening that not so profitable business that they always wanted. For others it is taking a hobby and turning it into a home-based business. Finally there are the people who pursued a career in an industry or company that offered good pay but little satisfaction. It is not uncommon for these people to give up the high paying salaries for lesser paying but more satisfying careers. I know of schoolteachers who were corporate attorneys and executives in their previous careers. But the fact is that only 1% of retirees have the life they had imagined while they were working.

Ability, Not Security

This is how Believers generate real security. They do not expect nor ask their employers, the government, or anyone else to provide it for them. They take responsibility for their own lives by retaining the power of deciding where they will arrive in life. They become the CEOs of their lives and this is a power that most employees sacrifice in order to have the insecurity of "job security."

CHAPTER SEVEN
Become a CEO

The real freedom of any individual can always be measured by the amount of responsibility which he must assume for his own welfare and security
–Robert Welch (1899-1985)

Due to the manner in which Believers view employment they either consciously or subconsciously develop a concept that I call being the CEO of their lives. This concept came to me when, after taking several business classes, I realized that life is like a business. Debt management and asset building is finance while the tracking of income and expenses is accounting. The proper and efficient administration of life, including resources, is business or operational management and the capacity to earn money is dependent on one's ability to market themselves.

This realization embedded itself into my consciousness and I could not help but ponder its meaning and how it affects our lives. The more I meditated on it the more it became clear to me that each of our lives are not only like a businesses, but that we are the Chief Executive Officers. This epiphany made me realize that, like all CEOs, we are each responsible for any and all successes and/or failures in our lives. This means that you are the one who has the final word in what happens in your life and although you may allocate some of the responsibility to others in the end you are the only one accountable for the results.

This does not suggest that you go it alone. On the contrary it is your responsibility as a good CEO to find qualified individuals to help and guide you with the operations of your life. These people should be experts in their field and have more knowledge on their specific subject than you do. It is very important that they should be ready to advise and educate you; not to make the decisions for you. In other words I learned to look at the experts whether they be financial, medical, or any other specialty as consultants. Their advice and recommendations are just that, advice and recommendations. You must fully understand what they are asking you to do because advisers and consultants are usually not around to see the outcome of following their advice.

Imagine yourself being the CEO of a company and these consultants were coming to you with the recommendations. You are responsible to sign off on each of them, which mean that you are physically putting your name and your reputation for each and everything you approve. Would you be willing to just turn everything over to them and trust that it will all come out okay? Or would you be a little bit more cautious and want to review the recommendations, maybe get a second opinion or increase your own knowledge on the subject matter? This is the same as your life except that it's not just your reputation that is at risk; it is your livelihood.

The reality is that you can never blindly accept the recommendation of any expert no matter who they are. I have seen financial advisors recommend investments that did help the clients but were neither the best nor the most efficient for what the client was trying to achieve. In many cases the product was recommended because the financial advisor received a higher commission for the sale. Another real case situation is when the advisor has all the best intentions but management is putting pressure to move a certain product such as life insurance. In this case the financial advisor may recommend a life insurance product that, again, does the job but has higher fees and more restrictions than a regular mutual fund.

The expert's lack of experience or knowledge may also hamper the recommendation. The fact is that experts can be just as wrong as a layman. In his book *Fighter Pilot* Paul Richey recounts his time in the RAF during World War II. He was stationed with a Hurricane squadron in France prior to the German invasion of 1940. He and his squadron mates realized the weakness of not having armor behind the pilot seat. This disadvantage allowed the enemy's bullets to almost decapitate the flyer as it passed through the plane. They sent a memo detailing the need for armor protection for the pilot to London. This memo was discussed by the experts at the Air Ministry and at Hawker Aircraft, the manufacturer of the plane. All the experts concurred that it was impossible to put armor plating behind the pilot since it would throw off the aircraft's center of gravity thus making the plane unstable and reduce its maneuverability. Unwilling to accept the wisdom of the experts the squadron removed the protective plating from another type of aircraft and adapted it to a Hurricane. Several test flights showed that the flight characteristics of the Hurricane was unchanged by the modification. The plane was then flown to London and from that point on all Hurricanes had protective armor that saved hundreds of pilots and was a contributing factor in the RAF's victory in the Battle of Britain.

The amount of time they have in their profession is also no indicator of how much faith you should have in their recommendations. About four years ago I had a phone call from a client whose brother-in-law was a financial advisor with more than 20 years experience and a very large and successful practice.

"John" my client started, "my brother-in-law wants to buy investment properties but he wants to do it with me because he is unfamiliar with them as investments."

"Hmm" I said, "that is pretty scary."

"I know" he replied, "What do you think I should do?"

"That's not what's scary." I explained, "What is scary is that your brother-in-law has been giving investment advice for over 20 years and he does not even have the most basic knowledge or experience with the number one wealth building investment in this country. That is what is scary."

I just cannot help but imagine what the advisor's recommendation to people was when they came to see him with an opportunity to buy an income producing property. Did he tell them that he had limited or no knowledge on the subject matter and recommend that they see an expert more qualified than he or, for fear of showing his lack of knowledge and possibly losing a sale, convinced these people that real estate is not a very good investment and that he could recommend something better? I also wonder how his clients reacted. I am sure very few of them even questioned his wisdom and sought further assistance. Since he was the expert most of them probably just turned their money over to him without any questions.

As a financial advisor I have seen countless times where people gave me their money and somehow felt they have done their part, leaving me to make the decisions. I often have to remind them that I never forget whose money it is and neither should they. If they still do not understand the point I am trying to make I usually try to drive it home with this remark:

"If I lose your money I will feel bad, but not as bad as you."

This usually enlightens them of their responsibility but, to my amazement, there are always a few who just don't get it.

Just like any business the management of our lives can determine whether we are successes or failures. As CEO it is your responsibility to see that every department in your business runs as efficiently as possible. If the accounting department, for example, is not providing you with the information you need to maintain a fiscally stable enterprise then you need to make changes in that department. This may require you to educate yourself in order to become more proficient in bookkeeping and accounting or, if this is beyond your abilities, you may wish to hire someone more qualified.

Your First Step as a CEO

One of the most important tasks that a CEO has is to define the company and its purpose. This definition gives focus to the company's activities and explains where, when, and how it is going to direct its energy. It ensures that all the employees are on the same page and working towards the same goals. This is done by developing a Mission or Vision Statement that becomes a roadmap of the company's future by laying out the direction the company is headed, the business position it intends to take, and the capabilities it has and intend to develop.

If properly implemented and communicated the statement can create a corporate culture and synergy that leads to efficiency within all parts of the company. If not created or implemented the business can find itself losing its focus and scattering its resources and energy into several non-productive directions. Instead of a laser guided shot to the bull's eye it is like using a shotgun and hoping enough of the shot will hit their target. In many cases it does not even know what or where the target is and is thus shooting blindly.

Unfortunately this is the approach most take with their lives. Too few give any thought about what they want out of their lives or where they want to go and how they are going to get there. Most pass through life on some form of autopilot that does not require them to think about or to make conscience decisions about what their lives really mean. With little thought they spend a great part of their waking hours going through motions that have been predetermined for them. They follow their compatriots on predictable well-trodden paths that promise bright futures but very often never deliver as promised.

> Vision without action is a daydream. Action with without vision is a nightmare.
> -Japanese Proverb

There is no better example of this than the one offered by the then Senator Barak Obama. In a 30-minute ad for his campaign he highlighted some of the suffering, uncertainty, and difficulty Americans were feeling during this economic crisis. One of those profiled was a young man working for the Ford Motor Corporation whose job and financial well-being was in serious jeopardy. The implication of the piece was that this man's father and grandfather had worked for the company and, like some sort of legacy, he was somehow entitled to a job there also. The inference being that somehow a promise was being broken for this 3rd generation autoworker.

It seems to me that this man's current situation is not the result of Ford or the United States government breaking a promise but of the worker taking a path of least resistance. Like most legacies he probably followed in his father and grandfather's footsteps because it was easier than seeking and making his own way through life. He failed to discover his purpose, vision, or calling in life. Instead he went through the motions while believing in promises that may not always come true.

I do not condemn this man since it is what most of us do. In the previous chapter on religion I discussed the importance that the Calvinists put on discovering their calling or purpose in life. I would not be surprised if 95% of those who read that chapter have no idea nor have given any thought to what their purpose is. This is tragic since the outcome of this lack of thinking can have a severe and harmful impact on our lives. In 1979 a study was conducted on the students of Harvard's MBA program. Through that study researchers found that only 13% had life goals and only 3% had actually put them into a written plan. The other 84% were going through the motions with no goals at all.

Researches then followed up with these students ten years later and while the results are not surprising the degree to which planning impacted their lives is. As would be expected the 13% that had goals were found to me making double of what the 84% without goals were making. The unexpected part was that the three percent that put their goals in writing and developed plans to achieve their goals were, on average, making ten times as much as the 97% combined.

This makes it clear that while one can get by without thinking about their purpose and goals in life it does make it nearly impossible to develop the abilities needed to succeed in life as well as to survive its less desirable events. This is why I think it is crucial to develop your own personal Mission/Vision statement. The first-step is to understand what such a statement should look like and below are two examples from the corporate world.

Microsoft:
One vision drives everything we do: A computer on every desk and in every home using great software as an empowering tool.

American Red Cross:
The mission of the American Red Cross is to improve the quality of human life; to enhance self-reliance and concern for others; and to help people avoid, prepare for, and cope with emergencies.

These are very typical vision statements and I ask you to note that nowhere in the statement do they mention profit or money as a goal. This is because they understand that money and profits come from providing services and products that meets people's wants and needs. Also note that it focuses the company's energy into a defined direction and activities. Keep this in mind as you develop your personal vision statement.

Next you need to look into yourself to discover your purpose. To do this I want you to take two to three days (yes, days) and ponder this question:

If money was no obstacle and I was guaranteed to succeed what would I do?

At first this may be difficult answer as nothing comes to you immediately. Do not give up, you have been ignoring yourself for most of your life and it may take time to re-establish communication. I am sure the seeds are there, you just need to discover them. The best place to start is your childhood when you use to dream of all the possibilities rather than thinking of all the impossibilities. Before you became tainted by the fear, the doubt, and the mistrust of yourself that adults refer to as being "practical and reasonable." Before the joy of living gave away to the responsibility of surviving.

> What is it that you, as a child, lived for?
> What gave you the greatest joy?
> The greatest satisfaction?
> What did you naturally excel at?

And now,
> What would you like to live for?
> What activity gives you the greatest joy?
> What are you a natural at?
> Finally, how are you going to make your mark in this world?

The more you ponder the more active your brain will become and, with a little effort, you will find yourself surprised by the power of your own thoughts. It is very important that you write down all answers your brain gives you to these questions no matter how ridicules or outrages they may appear. This is especially true if they come in the form of an epiphany or inspirations. Since these thoughts originate in the super-conscious, which is the most ignored part of the brain, they are the genesis of your mission from which you can create your Vision Statement. Once this has been accomplished try to write a basic statement on the next page

Warning: Your statement should encompass all aspects in your life and how you want to live your life in general. In a following chapter I will show you how to create plans for specific areas in your life.

My mission or vision of my life is...

CHAPTER EIGHT
The Real Danger of Risk

Security is mostly a superstition. It does not exist in nature, nor do the children of men as a whole experience it. Avoiding danger is no safer in the long run than outright exposure. The fearful are caught as often as the bold. Faith alone defends.
-Helen Keller (1880-1968)

In today's world of comfort and security "risk" is akin to a four-letter word and is to be avoided at all cost. Just to mention that there is risk, or even a remote possibility of a setback, in something that can cause many people to shut down and not hear anything that follows. Many people want a "sure thing" that does not involve any amount of uncertainty, no matter how slight, and is guaranteed. By playing it safe and staying within their comfort zone they believe they are minimizing the chances of something bad happening. This thinking is very dangerous and more often leads to less than desirable if not tragic results than the more "risky" alternatives.

Helen Keller's quote insightfully highlights that safety is a figment of our imagination and that risk or danger can never be completely avoided. No matter how hard people try to be "safe than sorry" they are still just as likely to be caught by events that have negative impacts on their lives. The truth of the matter is that we cannot control what happens in the world beyond ourselves. A person can be the ideal employee but economic factors, such a global outsourcing, can leave that person unemployed and without income. The healthiest of people can be stricken with cancer or a stroke that leaves their body broken and, with today's healthcare cost, their bank account depleted. Even the greatest "security blanket" of them all, money in the bank, can quickly be drained by a major event.

This is something that Believers accept as fact and find those who seek safety as being delusional. The Believers understand that the best they can hope for in life is not to eliminate risk but to develop the physical, psychological, and emotional abilities to handle the dangers of living. This changes their focus from trying to be safe to being prepared for the uncertainties of life. Education, self-development, and independence take on an urgent significance as they recognize the potential threats around them and strive to be as prepared as possible to meet any that may materialize. Believers also realize that taking risk is required if one is to protect one's self. This is confirmed in Dr. Thomas Stanley's book the Millionaire Mind when he discovered that 41% of self-made millionaires believe that the willingness to take financial risk is very important to one's financial success.

> The worst sorrows in life are not its losses and misfortunes, but its fears.
> – Arthur Christopher Benson

When comparing the approaches of the Doubters and the Believers I am reminded of a dinner meeting I had a couple of years ago. I was in a restaurant with several people and for about an hour or so we had been discussing the philosophy of gaining independence. When the food arrived the conversation became more intimate as groups of two or three began to discuss the various topics amongst themselves.

At this point the lady across the table from me pointed across the room and asked me, "Do you see that woman sitting in the over there?"

"Yes", I replied.

"She works with me and she is very interested in what we're doing", my dinner partner continued. "But she is afraid to get involved because she doesn't want to do anything risky."

"Risky," I excitedly replied, "What does she do now that is not risky?"

"Well," the woman replied, "as I said she works with me and has been doing so for the last 10 years. She puts money into our company 401(k) plan

> There is no security on earth, there is only opportunity.
> - General Douglas MacArthur (1880-1964)

and about two years ago she and her husband bought a house that they hope to have paid off by the time they retire. So right now she feels pretty secure and doesn't want to do anything that might jeopardize their plans"

After a few seconds of thinking it dawned on me how much in jeopardy their plans already are and I shared this revelation with my guest.

"Because I understand the true dangers that living life involves I have developed abilities that give me the confidence to succeed in life. I know that all does not go well so therefore I do not fall victim to a false sense of security. Over the years I have developed knowledge that, if for some bizarre reason, I should lose everything I have acquired I know that I would be able to regain my lost wealth within a few short years."

I then continued, "Her way, 'the secure way', is to obediently go to work every day, make contributions out of every paycheck to her retirement plan, and plan to pay off her house by the time she retires. That sounds pretty good but it is all dependent on her and her husband's income, which is in the hands of her employer and at the mercies of not just the national job market but also the global market since most jobs can now be outsourced. The retire plan must perform as expected, but it is in the hands of fund managers and at the mercies of the market. Also her home will need to appreciate at a constant rate if she expects it to supplement her retirement. The danger she is taking is that very little of her plan is actually in her hands; she has hardly any control over what happens. I do not know about you but her plan sounds a lot more risky than mine. She just better cross her fingers and pray that nothing goes wrong over the next 30 or so years."

> The way to be safe is never to be secure.
>
> - Benjamin Franklin (1706-1790)

Unfortunately this is the approach most people take and they foolishly believe they are "safe" because it appears that way. They tend to focus on the immediate, but often benign, short-term risk at the expense of recognizing and dealing with the more severe danger of the long-term risk. "People all over the country," they tell themselves, "do this without any problems so it must be the right path." What they do not realize is that Doubters make up the majority of the population and this is the common path that they take in life. They include such a huge number of people that it appears that only a small percentage suffer from the dangers in life. In reality, since so very few are Believers, proportionately the play-it-safers suffer more and in the end are less well off than their "bold/risky" compatriots. I'll repeat the fact that only four to five percent of people retire financially independent enough not to be a burden on the government or their families and I can state with confidence that very few if any of them are Doubters who preferred to be safe than sorry. The irony is that in the end they are sorry.

At the time of the writing of this chapter an economic crisis threatens the livelihood of each and every one of us. After several months of increasing unemployment, bank closures, record oil prices and home foreclosures, government bailouts, and a weakening dollar the economic decline that was started by the bursting of the housing market has found its way into the general economy. Many average Americans who thought they were on the well-beaten path to safety are losing their homes and their jobs. What they did not realize is that the path to safety is full of hidden pitfalls and has a mythical unreachable destination.

I do not know what will happen in respects to the economy but I do know that it will either get better or become worse and, if it does get worse, many believe that there is a real danger of another great depression. If this does come to pass everyone will be affected. No job will be safe and a new one will be hard to find. Credit markets will dry up and even the best credit scores will be meaningless. Without income and loans many people will not be able to maintain their lifestyles as they lose those items that they purchased with credit such as their automobiles and homes. People not affected will see their investments shrink as more and more people drain their savings and then their retirement plans in an attempt to save themselves. Those who carefully planned every step and played it safe by avoiding risk may find themselves just as destitute as the most aggressive risk-taker. Helen Keller's words ring true as the crisis catches the "fearful" along with the "bold."

If we are lucky we may dodge the bullet this time but take note that depressions can and do happen. Just because this one does not come to pass it does not mean that depressions are a thing of the past, like some sort of economic dinosaur. Since 1800 this great nation has suffered six depressions with three of them considered severe or great and the last starting in 1929. That is six in the last 200 years and the last one was almost 80 years ago. You do the math. "But John", I am told, "we are more sophisticated, more knowledgeable, more savvy than our predecessors. We have learned from their mistakes and now have institutions that regulate and control the economy. They'll prevent a depression from happening again." This is true and it has worked for almost 80 years but, like all economics systems that attempt to regulate, it can never be 100% foolproof. We humble humans need to accept that some things are just beyond our control. If we did have that capacity we would not be in the situation we currently find ourselves in.

So it is very important to ask yourself, "If and when the depression hits will you be ready?" I am not talking financially since, as I explained in the chapter on money, this can quickly be drained. What I am talking about is having the faith and self-confidence required to see you through such severe economic times. When you and your family have lost everything (your home, your cars, your livelihood) will you have the mental, emotional, and spiritual strength to carry on? If you do wallow through will you be a stronger person or a broken shell of the person you once were?

In the last depression many did not have what it took. This was especially true for those who thought they were immune from the danger since they avoided taking risk. They had listened and obeyed all the words of caution and conventional wisdom that was suppose to protect them from suffering such a fate. In the end they became gripped by fear, anxiety, and worry. With their decision-making abilities clouded they resorted to the time honored method of decision making, which was to follow the crowd. After a short time they discovered that these paths, clogged with the frightened and indecisive, were roads to nowhere. Not being able to think beyond the obvious they resigned themselves to the fact that they will need to turn to the government and charity to provide for their and their family's needs.

Many did survive those terrible times but they came out of it spiritually, psychologically, and emotionally scarred, if not broken, by their experiences. Others, unfortunately, were so full of doubt and lack of confidence that they could not even face the challenge they saw before them and preferred to take the cowardly why out. One of the most common images of the time was that of these Doubters leaping out of windows to their death. As we now know the Great Depression, like all crisis, was temporary and life not only went on but thrived during the decades that followed. But this came too late for the leapers. Their great depression became permanent.

So far the current crisis has been mild to the great one that started in 1929 but this does not stop Doubters from making deadly decisions. There have been several news reports of weak and fearful individuals taking their own lives and even those of others. Recently a client of mine called me and told me that she was helping a lady who, like many, lost her home to foreclosure. My client was allowing the lady to stay with her until she was able to

Danger of Risk

get back on her feet. Shortly after that my client went on vacation and while she was away the lady hung herself form the staircase. My client's eighteen year old daughter discovered the body when she returned home from work. What is amazing to me is that someone would kill themselves over a house. A HOUSE!! How pathetic is that!

Let us be clear as to the real motivation behind these cowardly and selfish acts. Most often it is assumed that the pressure from the financial setback caused the person to act the way he did. This is no truer than it is for the person who kills himself and/or his family because of a pending divorce. The truth is that, like divorce, there is life after a bankruptcy or foreclosure. During these times life may be difficult but it is not unbearable and definitely not fatal. Millions of people have gone on to live prosperous lives after experiencing these events (see page 110 for a few famous ones).

The real motivation is fear. But not the fear of losing all that they have achieved for this, especially material items like houses, can be replaced. It is the fear that all Doubters and Other-directed people dread the most: the fear of losing the approval of their peers. The lady above is a prime example. Knowing she was going to lose the house she had already found new accommodations. Being relatively young she also started working on building her post-foreclosure life. The problem came when her family started to criticize and ridicule her. She had been the only person in her peer group, including friends and family, to make an attempt at homeownership. In typical other-directed fashion the less ambitious members of her peer group became envious. Through this envy they saw her failed attempt to improve herself as an opportunity to "cut here down to size." It was the pressure from the group and her inability to resist their disapproval that drove her to take her own life..

It is my opinion that this is the main reason these people kill themselves. They cannot handle the disapproval of their peer group, which may include a combination of family, friends, co-workers, colleagues and associates. In order to illustrate why I think this to be true I'll change the circumstances that relate to the lady above. Lets assume that a natural disaster or some other event caused her to lose her home and that she was not compensated for the loss. Now lets see if it changes the response or outcome. Under these circumstances I do not believe that she would have killed herself. Although financially the results would be the same how she is viewed would change. In this scenario she would be seen as a victim, which is perfectly acceptable to her peer group. Instead of criticism and ridicule they would have rallied around her with love and support. Again, financially she would be no better of but she still would have had the approval of her peers. The tragedy here is that these people could not rise above their own fear and doubt to help this woman in her time of need. In the end it was the evilness of their envy and not money that destroyed this life.

As I write this part of the chapter I am waiting for a client at my favorite restaurant, TAPS in Corona, CA. I happen to look up and there is a man in a wheelchair. As I watched this man and his lady friend I come to the conclusion that he is a paraplegic and I assume he will be

> Success is not final, failure is not fatal; it is the courage to continue that matters.
> -Winston Churchill (1874-1965)

for life. Yet this man, with all the challenges he faces in life, gets up day after day and takes on whatever difficulties comes his way. While others kill themselves because, like some defeated samurai, they cannot endure the shame of losing people's approval. I must ask myself, "Who are the real cripples in this world?"

"Keep calm, for anxiety impairs judgment."

The above quote is from the memoirs of Squadron Leader Charles Demoulin, DFC who was a fighter pilot in the Royal Air Force (609 Squadron) during the violent years of World War II. It was a lesson he learned while facing the possibility of death in a fiery crash- or worse surviving a fiery crash only to be forever disfigured. Fortunately, after surviving several crash landings, a dozen hours floating wounded in the English Channel, and several months as a P.O.W. Squadron Leader Demoulin lived to share his experiences with us and, some forty years later, the knowledge gained over a lifetime. Not only was he a fighter pilot, he also trained and led other men into the deadly European skies. He learned a truth that very few people truly understand and that truth is that anxiety, nervousness, worry, apprehension, and fear affect our ability to judge situations correctly and to make the best decisions.

Believers do this by accepting the fact that things do go wrong in life and one just has to deal with it. By doing so they are seldom caught by surprise because they are constantly examining what could go wrong. This allows them to be more capable of handling negative situations and, by examining all their options regardless of its practicality or what others think, be more responsive. They often have both short-term and long-term options prepared in the event something happens. The short-term options provide an immediate quick fix to a problem while the long-term solutions look beyond the immediate problem and, if possible, provide a solution that will reduce the chances of it happening again or at least limiting the harm it causes.

This mental exercise is beneficial in many ways. It helps them be prepared for most foreseeable circumstances by having contingency plans in place. This in turn reduces the stress they suffer when negative events do happen and they are able to maintain a positive attitude by retaining the sense that they have control over what is happening. By doing so they are able to avoid the helplessness many feel during these times and minimize the frustration they can feel. Finally a person can be either optimistic or pessimistic but not both. By always having something positive to do they minimizes the possibility that they will become despondent or depressed.

The result is that they are able to follow Squadron Leader Demoulin's admonition and remain calm during difficult situations. This allows them to be clear headed as they analyze the situation and map out their strategy to get through and then out of the crisis. They are able to focus on out-of-the-box options that provide long-term solutions not just knee-jerk reactions that provide nothing but short-term band-aids. It keeps them a Believer and they avoid the harmful thinking of the Doubters.

When I speak on this subject I usually get the response that somehow I am different than the other people and that I have the internal strength and composure to remain calm during difficult times. They say that they cannot help but be stressed or worried or anxious when things do not go as planned. I reply that I have not always been this way. As a child I was afraid to do anything that may cause me harm and it was not until I joined the Army that the idea that I am capable of more than I believed came

Danger of Risk

to plant itself in my mind. This grew over time as I was tested by life's ups and downs but it was my father who finally gave me the lesson I needed to learn.

It happened when I was in my twenties. I had invested a small but then valuable sum of money. Unfortunately the investment did not turn out as planned. Feeling down and desperate I called my dad with the hope that he may be of some help. After I was done explaining what had happened, my dad started laughing. Here I was totally stressed out and my dad is laughing at me. I told him that I did not think it was funny and to this day I have never forgotten what came next.

"John", he said, "it is only money, don't worry about it. You cannot change what happened and it does no good to fixate on it. Just focus on what you are going to do next."

"But what about the money I lost?" I inquired.

"Did you learn something from this?" He asked.

"Yeah, I guess so", I replied.

To which in a matter of fact manner he responded, "Then consider it the price of tuition."

In my mind's eye I can still see, like a movie, how that conversation played out. I can remember how panicked I felt, my dad laughing at me, and his reply. Even though I did not realize it at the time my dad laughing at me was the best thing he could have done. He put the event in its perspective place and I got through the "crisis" unscathed

> A life spent making mistakes is not only more honorable but more useful than a life spent doing nothing.
>
> - George Bernard Shaw (1856-1950)

which increased the faith I have in myself. I also learned that, although they may appear to be so, most bad circumstances, unless they are life threatening, do not mark the end of the world and with time end up being speed bumps on the road of life.

From this I learned to take action by focusing on the solution rather than the problem and to avoid worrying about what happened. I also learned that worrying is not concern or deep thinking. It is a state of self-pity where people fixate on what has happened, why it happened, and most importantly, why did it have to happen to them. It has been my observation that the people who worry are more likely people who lack decision-making abilities. Author Kathleen McGowen confirms these observations in her novel *The Expected One* in which she writes:

> Success is going from failure to failure without loss of enthusiasm.
> - Winston Churchill (1874-1965)

"There's no stopping the habitual worrier. Studies of worriers show that fretting actually makes them less anxious -- at least while they're in the midst of it. That's because worrying gives the illusion of control. You think that by imagining all the worst things that could happen, you can have solutions in place beforehand. But the reality is that since you'll never think of all the possibilities, your worrying work is never done."

In other words the worrying replaces them having to take the actions and responsibilities required to find a solution to the problem. In their mind they believe that worrying about the problem is dealing with it even though nothing productive comes from this activity and it greatly impairs their judgment.

Danger of Risk

A few months ago I was having a meeting with a couple, Bob and Suzy, who are clients of mine. Some how we got on the subject of responsibility and Suzy stated that, "Bob is very irresponsible". Having known them for several years I was a little surprised by the remark.

"It seems to me Bob is like a fireman," I replied. " He seems to always putting out one brushfire or another. I do not see where he is 'irresponsible'".

"Oh, he does," she said, "but he does not take things seriously."

"I still do not understand," I said. "How can he take things anymore seriously then taking care of the problems as they arise?"

At this point Bob jumped in. "Let me explain. Suzy comes from a family of worriers. They worry over everything no matter how big or how small. I've come to the conclusion that they just like to worry. It makes them feel like they are doing something important; that they are 'serious' about life. But yet nothing ever changes for them. Worrying has become a means onto itself.

"I was brought up different. I was taught that there is never a good reason to worry. If you can do something about a problem, don't worry! Fix the problem! If you can't do anything about a problem don't worry because it will not change anything. The ironic part of this is that I fix the problems while she worries and I am the 'irresponsible' one."

I knew what Bob was talking about because I know what worrying, anxiety and other like responses to problems truly are. They are manipulative tools that people use to relieve themselves of responsibility while giving the essence of being responsible. I recommend that you give up the worrying habit because it self-indulgent, irresponsible, immature and does more harm than good.

Only Faith Defends

Those who have achieved financial independence appear to agree with the above statement by Helen Keller. In a survey of millionaires conducted by Dr. Thomas Stanley "Believing in myself" was the number one reason to explain why they were able to overcome their fears and achieve success. This is the faith Helen Keller was referring to. It is not only the faith we have in our abilities as mentioned above but also the understanding that we are not perfect and will make mistakes that can cause us harm. Doubters see these mistakes as personal failures and the resulting negative self-criticism only leads to them to quit. This reinforces the belief that they are losers and forces them to completely avoid all risk. Their lives become stagnant and the joys of living become almost nonexistent. Their self-worth diminishes and they develop a sense of being helpless, unable to control what happens to them. They come to see themselves as victims of circumstance without the ability to change undesirable situations. Doubt and fear darkens their hearts and leaves them with only one goal in life: to get through it with as little difficulty as possible. With their spirits broken life becomes something that they try to survive rather than something they live.

> A smooth sea never made a skilled mariner.
> -English Proverb

Believers do not have rock solid confidence that does not get shaken or fractured by the events in their lives. What they do have is the capacity and knowledge to quickly recover their self-confidence. One of the reasons for this is that they accept setbacks as a normal part of living. This approach helps them to avoid seeing these setbacks as personal failures. Instead they regard them as learning experiences. If they should fail Believers, rather than beating themselves up with negative self-defeating criticism, step back and begin to search for a solution. While they do examine what went wrong, it is more of an academic exercise from which lessons are learned and done only after a workable solution has been found and implemented.

This is what sets them apart from Doubters. Where Doubters focus on the problem by lamenting their situation or feeling sorry for themselves Believers focus on finding a solution. Once successfully out of the quagmire they are ever more confident in their abilities. Even if the problem was caused by an action they took Believers still maintain their positive mindset by focusing on the solution and not beating themselves over their mistake. This allows Believers to keep things in perspective and it has been my experience that more often than not it will lead to encountering the means to repair the resultant damage. In other words they become better not bitter from their failures.

There is no substitute for experience and this is especially true in regards to faith and confidence. They can only be gained through a trial of fire. The biggest determinant of our confidence is how we handle our failures. As we accept risk and face challenges we will make errors and mistakes but, with perseverance and determination, we overcome obstacles our confidence increases. Contrarily our faith and confidence is reduced each time we run away from a challenge. The shame and self-pity that comes from quitting as soon as our attempts meet failure prevents us from growing and developing. By not taking on and overcoming life's small challenges we never develop the abilities to effectively handle the larger ones.

Developing confidence or faith in one's abilities creates an independence and immunity that Doubters can never achieve. By deciding if we are we going to become better or bitter as a result of those failures we are deciding if we are going to be Believers or Doubters. If we decide to become better then we can usually persevere and overcome. We soon begin to have faith in ourselves and in our abilities to handle life's difficulties. On the other hand as the illustrations shows by avoiding risk we never develop the attitude and abilities needed to care for ourselves when dangers arise. Life becomes something to survive through rather than to live.

Personal Development & Risk

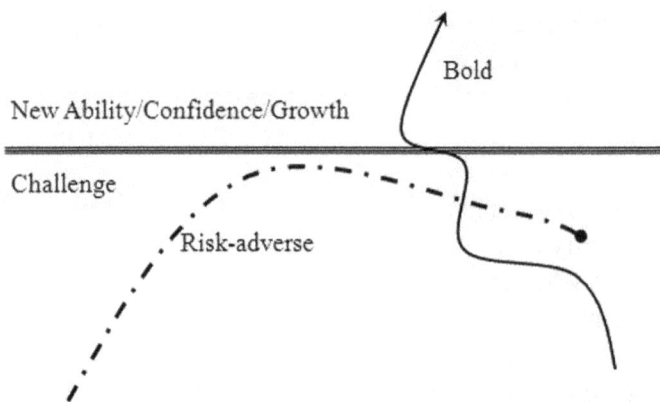

As this faith grows you will move from being a Doubter to a Believer. Life will become richer and fuller as you develop into a competent and successful individual. Finally, you will be able to read the poem below and say to yourself, yes I am.

Danger of Risk

"If"
by Rudyard Kipling

If you can keep your head when all about you
Are losing theirs and blaming it on you,
If you can trust yourself when all men doubt you
But make allowance for their doubting too,
If you can wait and not be tired by waiting,
Or being lied about, don't deal in lies,
Or being hated, don't give way to hating,
And yet don't look too good, nor talk too wise:
If you can dream--and not make dreams your master,
If you can think--and not make thoughts your aim;
If you can meet with Triumph and Disaster
And treat those two impostors just the same;
If you can bear to hear the truth you've spoken
Twisted by knaves to make a trap for fools,
Or watch the things you gave your life to, broken,
And stoop and build 'em up with worn-out tools:
If you can make one heap of all your winnings
And risk it all on one turn of pitch-and-toss,
And lose, and start again at your beginnings
And never breath a word about your loss;
If you can force your heart and nerve and sinew
To serve your turn long after they are gone,
And so hold on when there is nothing in you
Except the Will which says to them: "Hold on!"
If you can talk with crowds and keep your virtue,
Or walk with kings--nor lose the common touch,
If neither foes nor loving friends can hurt you;
If all men count with you, but none too much,
If you can fill the unforgiving minute
With sixty seconds' worth of distance run,
Yours is the Earth and everything that's in it,
And--which is more--you'll be a Man, my son!

Not All Bankruptcies Are Equal

Nothing puts more fear into the heart of a Doubter than financial loss since it strikes at their all to important sense of security. To them nothing is more catastrophic than financial ruin and, of course, their prestige along with their self-worth would be tarnished. Believers know that the worst that can happen is bankruptcy, which does not have any permanent effect, and that all bankruptcies are not created equal. Believers understand three different causes of bankruptcy.

- **Irresponsible Stupidity**: Extravagant spending on non-appreciating goods such as cars, clothes, electronic gadgets, usually for the purpose of impressing others.

- **Unexpected Circumstances**: BK caused when an unexpected economic or medical crisis occurs due to no fault of the individual.

- **Failed Attempt to Better One's Position**: This includes starting a business, incurring student loans on an education that does not payoff, etc.

Only the first one negatively reflects on a person's character and judgment. The others may or may not depending on the overall circumstances. Some may believe the last one may reflect bad judgment but most Believer understand that success is not a straight path and failure is just part of the learning process. On the next page I list several famous people whose first attempts at success ended as financial failures and bankruptcy but who incredibly went on to become very successful.

> **Note:** I am not promoting the notion that Bankruptcy is nothing to concern yourself with. What I am saying is that, as these individuals prove, it is not a life-ending event. It is a difficult thing to go through and there are consequences to filing for bankruptcy but the effects are temporary. If you believe that you can make something of your life but it will require taking some risk do not let your fear of BK stop you. As I always say:
>
> "I rather take some risk and make a mistake while I still have the time and energy to repair it than to play it safe all my life only to find that that was the biggest mistake of all and now I do not have the time or energy to do anything about it."

True Winners Succeed After Failure

PT Barnum (1810-1891): Filed BK after failed business venture. Went on to establish Barnum & Bailey Circus and is now considered a business genius.

Henry John Heinz (1844-1919): First condiment company filed BK in 1875. Learned from his mistakes and started Heinz 57, which is still a very successful business to this day.

Milton S. Hershey (1857-1945): Started 4 companies that all ended as failures in BK court. His fifth attempt with chocolates was a great success and he even has a town named after him.

Henry Ford (1863-1947): Established three automobile manufacturing companies of which the first two were failures and he filed for BK. The last was the well known Ford Motor Co. that is still producing cars for the drivers of the world.

Walt Disney (1901-1966): Filed BK in 1920 due to failed business. Went on to create Mickey Mouse and the Disney Empire.

Donald Trump (1946-): Twice, in 1992 and 2004, his casino businesses filed for Chapter 11 bankruptcy. "The Donald" is still going strong and is often considered America's #1 businessman.

CHAPTER NINE
Do Not Be Afraid, Be Prepared

Luck is what happens when preparation meets opportunity.
         -Seneca (ca. 500 AD)

In the previous chapter we saw that by striving for security and avoiding risk we expose ourselves to the real danger of being lulled into a false sense of security and becoming complacent. For too many of us our education and development lose their importance once we gain a desirable level of comfortable and perceived "security." This attitude leaves us grossly unprepared when a crisis occurs. By attempting to avoid risk and the chance of failure, we do not develop the abilities and emotional strength to effectively handle it when it happens.

Furthermore, since we never really challenge ourselves, we are never quite sure of what we are truly capable of. This creates uncertainty in ourselves thus preventing us from having the faith that Keller says is required to defend from danger. This leads us to live in fear and having to relying on others such as employers, unions, the government, etc to provide security for us. This lack of faith and dependency on others for our well-being reduces the amount of control we have over our lives. It is this lack of control combined with the self-doubt we have in our individual abilities is the real danger of seeking security rather that preparedness.

In this chapter I will help you start to develop the confidence and faith that Helen Keller says is needed. Being prepared is essential and I believe that Seneca was seeing only half of what luck is. The other half of luck that he does not recognize is what happens when disaster is avoided or minimized by being prepared. Like the luck a family has when all its members escape unharmed from a burning home because they had a plan or the luck of a police officer being able to return to home to his family because he had worn a bulletproof vest. I am now going to help you make a plan and a bulletproof vest that will help you with the fires and projectiles that life throws at you.

In the last chapter I alluded to a method I use to avoid being lulled in to a false sense of security. This method helps me to be as prepared as possible to prevent or minimize the effect of the negative events that can pass in my life. It is derived from an exercise I learned in my business management class and is used by businesses to study possible marketing strategies. It is called a S.W.O.T. analysis and with a few changes I find it just as useful in my personal life.

The S.W.O.T. acronym stands for:

Strengths
Weaknesses
Opportunities
Threats

You start by folding a piece of paper twice so that it has four squares and then label each square one of the above titles. So your paper should look at this.

Strengths	Opportunities
Weaknesses	Threats

The second step is to fill in each box. I like to start by focusing on a specific threat and in this example I will use Job/Income loss. I then begin to analyze my strengths, weaknesses, and opportunities. In the strengths box I list what I currently have going for me. In the weakness box I write the items that may permit the threat to happen and, if it does, what will prevent me from minimizing its impact of my life. In the opportunities box I can list what I can do now with the strengths I currently possess to reduce the weaknesses I have. So, for example, if you want to focus on your income/employment your paper may now look like this:

Strengths	Opportunities
Currently Employed Stable Income Educated Skilled Experienced	Possibility for Advancement
Weaknesses	**Threats**
Not up to date on new technology Education can be better Hate the boss/company/work Resume not prepared Job can be outsourced Pay high relative to market Common skills/education Lack of management/leadership experience Dependent on job	Job/income loss

Finally, the Threat box helps you identify what can go wrong. The Weakness box highlights areas where you have a deficiency that may compound the effects of the threat.

The Opportunities box can help you see what is available to you and can provide a solution to a weakness such as a lack of management experience. The items listed in your Strength box can be used to create your resume or to highlight to your employer why you deserve to advance within the company. You may actually be surprised by how strong you are and that you may have more going for you then you think.

You now you have a list that you can proactively work from to prepare yourself in case the threat becomes real. This will help you from getting caught unaware and knowing that you are prepared for these potentially harmful events gives you a sense of control over your life. Just remember you do not need to tackle all the weaknesses at once. You can start on the smaller and simpler ones like preparing a current resume and work your way to the more difficult and time-consuming items on the list.

The beauty of this exercise is that you can use it for just about all aspects of your life and combining it with the Vision Statement you developed in chapter 7 it becomes a very powerful tool that can literally change your life. All you need to do is write your Vision Statement at the top of the page and go through each box. Try to make it as detailed as possible and do not limit yourself. Once completed you will know where you stand, where you have to go, and what you have to do to achieve the vision you have for your life. Do not worry if it looks overwhelming or impossible just start with the doable items and as you grow so will your abilities to overcome the bigger items.

This can also be used for more specific areas of your life such as work, family, health, relationships, etc. As you think about each box write down everything that comes to you. Do not hesitate to write items down even if they seem incredible, impossible, or unlikely. We often have the tendency to limit our thinking by underestimating and doubting ourselves and minimizing events we do not want to happen. Do not do this. First of all anything is possible and even the most dreadful of events can happen. Secondly, you have more going for you then you believe! I have yet to meet a worthless person I am sure that if I met you this will not change.

One of the other benefits of this exercise is that it can be used to help with goal setting and the achievement of those goals. The only difference is which square we focus on. For example, we had been married for about a year and were expecting our first child. I was working full-time and taking a full load at the local university. I needed to update my computer but money was tight. So I sat down and used the S.W.O.T. analysis to see if I could find a solution. The first one I did was titled "How can I use my computer to make money?" I focused on my strengths and weaknesses with the hope that they would point me into the right direction and it looked like this.

How can I make money using my computer?

Strengths	Opportunities
Accounting & Financial Education Knowledge of Accounting Software Knowledge of Basic tax Preparation Knowledge of tax principles	
Weaknesses Limited time Limited money Need flexibility No credentials or professional certifications	

By focusing on my strengths I was able to come up with two alternatives, which I listed in the opportunities box.

How can I make money using my computer?

Strengths	Opportunities
Accounting & Financial Education Knowledge of Accounting Software Knowledge of Basic tax Preparation Knowledge of tax principles	Bookkeeping Services Tax Preparation Services
Weaknesses Limited time Limited money Need flexibility No credentials or professional certifications	

I now examined my weaknesses and realized that the bookkeeping service was not an option due to the limitations on my time. Tax preparation, on the other hand, would only be demanding for about ten weeks out of the year. I would be able to focus on my work, school, and family for the rest of the year. This analysis helped me make the best decision and I started my tax preparation business. Over the years that business has grown from making a few extra dollars doing basic returns to providing a large percentage of my annual income. I am now certified and it is a full service operation providing preparation services for corporations and partnerships as well as individuals.

If you wish to make this even more effective you can combine this tool with what is commonly referred to the "Tim Allen" method of goal achieving. Tim Allen, of *Home Improvement* fame, came up with this method while he was a struggling actor still trying to "make it" and he credits it as one of the keys to his success. He would set an annual goal that he wanted to achieve. This would be his master goal for the year and he would work on it by coming up with a supporting smaller goal that he could do each week. Then he did the same thing for a daily goal that helped him with the weekly goal. By breaking the larger goals down into smaller ones he was able to consistently work towards his life's dream on a daily basis.

In this case you will write your master goal in the Opportunity box and then in the Weakness box you can list the items that are preventing you from achieving that goal. By doing this you are breaking the larger goal down into smaller do-able steps. These steps will make up an action list that will become your weekly and daily goals. If you need to you can do the same exercise for your weekly goal in order to get your daily goals. Do not worry if some of the weaknesses seem impossible. Just start with the easiest and as you check off each one you will find your confidence, abilities, and faith increasing. This will give you the strength to take on the more difficult challenges and before long a seemingly impossible goal will be within your grasp.

More importantly this exercise will help you avoid the sense of helplessness, fear, and worry that overcome many during times of difficulty. The lists that are created will always provide you with positive and productive activities to do. You will be able to regain and maintain the amount of control you have in and over your life. If you work on the lists each day you will be able to rest assured at night knowing that although life maybe difficult you have taken positive steps in changing things for the better.

It is important to understand that your mind can only hold one thought at a time and if it is focusing on doing the positive then the negative and unproductive thoughts have no way to intrude themselves. Imagine that there are two beasts in your mind and they live off your thoughts. One is a good beast and the other is a bad beast. If we think positive thoughts the good beast gets stronger while the bad beast becomes weaker and we become positive people who start to believe in ourselves. But if we think negative thoughts then the bad beast soon takes control and doubt and fear will dominate. If you find yourself feeding the bad beast then all you need to do is to refocus your mental energy back to your list. By doing so you will be back feeding the good beast. The truth is that negative and unproductive thoughts can only enter your mind with your permission.

What normally happens is that in time you will need to do this exercise less and less. The reason for this is that:

1. You have achieved more and more of goals and
2. Your mind has been trained to do the analysis without doing the exercise.

When this happens you will have clarity of vision that will allow you to see the dangers and opportunities that are around you. In no time people will begin calling you "lucky." But you will know the truth: that unlike them you were prepared!

CHAPTER TEN
The Correct Education

If you believe you are born with all the smarts and gifts you'll ever have, you tend to approach life with a fixed mind-set. However, those who believe that their abilities can expand over time live with a growth mind-set—and they're much more innovative.
-Dr. Marshall Goldsmith

One day in January 1989 I was at my parent's dinner table busily filling out forms when my dad returned from one of his many doctor appointments. The month before I had come to live with my parents after spending several months in England and was preparing to return to school after a five-year hiatus. He had just been diagnosed with cancer of the larynx and at age fifty-nine his future looked bleak. He asked me what I was doing and I explained that I was registering with the local community college and was selecting my classes. With that he sat down and I returned to the papers I had in front of me.

A few minutes later he asked me what classes I was going to take. I explained that I wanted to get a degree in International Business but that I had to take my general education classes first. Also, since I have been out of school for so long, they were making me take remedial math and English classes. Seeming satisfied he nodded and I once again returned to my papers. Minutes passed silently until he unexpectedly stated that I should forget the degree and focus on the education. When I turned to him I must have had a very confused look on my face. My dad was a very educated man with an Engineering Degree from U.C.L.A. Furthermore, for all he had always stressed that the key to success was education so this seemed very out of character for him. I started to wonder if the radiation treatments were not impairing his ability to think.

"Degrees are important if you want to be dependent on someone else for your income. But most degrees only teach you how to work for money and nothing about having money work for you. Without the second part your livelihood will always be in the hands of others who really could care less what happens to you. I recommend that you get an education that allows you to provide for yourself and forget about the degree. Remember, a degree does not mean you are educated. There are a lot of uneducated people with degrees and there are, equally, a lot of very educated people who do not have degrees."

> I never let my schooling interfere with my education
> - Mark Twain (1835-1910)

Of course being a product of a society where symbolism is more important than substance I went for the degree while my dad triumphantly fought his battle with cancer. So it was not until fifteen years later that I understood what he told me that day. Once again cancer invaded his body and this time it was going to be the victor as it quickly destroyed him from within. We were at my brother's house where he and my mom were staying while my dad was receiving his treatments. I was with him as he sat in his wheelchair, feet and legs swollen beyond use by the radiation treatments.

My dad was enjoying one of his favorite snacks, celery with peanut butter, as another family member was proudly praising the accomplishments of her daughter who was away at university. "She is taking twenty units and instead of four years" exclaimed the proud mother, "she will have her degree in two and a half to three years." Recalling my days at school I had to think how much time could she be giving to each class and how much would she be getting out of those classes. I also realized that while the family member was talking about the degree she never mentioned the education that her daughter would receive. After she left I looked at my dad's deteriorated form and said, "It looks like getting the degree is more important that getting an education."

My dad responded with as much of a smile that he could muster and a slight nod in agreement. After some thought, with his mind still sharp, he raise his electronic voice box to his throat and said, "That is what I tried to tell you fifteen years ago and you did not listen. It is only now, after all these years of experience and seeing how people live, do you understand. Why do you think she should know any better?"

My dad was not only educated but also very enlightened and wise. I am not sure if it was his engineering background, his lifetime experience, a natural gift, or a combination of all three but he was able to distinguish between the symbol and what it represented. Like how he saw that money has no value, it is what it represents that has the value and how he saw that the difference between having a degree and being educated. This is something that the average person just cannot seem to do. They focus on the symbol rather than that which it represents. As a result the certificates on the walls, the clothes on the body, and the car that transports that body easily impresses them. What is interesting is that most successful Believers, like my dad, look beyond the superficial and examine what is in the mind, the heart, and the soul of that body.

Under that examination it appears that conventional education fall short and does not impress. Several years ago I met a very successful man who was gracious enough to share his story with me. After his tale of participating in both successful and unsuccessful endeavors he asked me, "You have a college degree, don't you?"

To which I replied, "Yes, I have a B.A."

"Well, you know what they say" he said with a little laughter and a twinkle in his eye, "The higher the degree the stupider you become. Of course I have always felt that that is not true. What happens is that the more 'educated' you become the less you are able to think independently. Everything is reduced to some prescribed formula and there is a prescribed way to respond. You stop trusting your natural instincts; your natural ability to think creatively and you end up thinking in a box. Much like a computer does. The creative benefit that we as humans are gifted with is completely suppressed, if not destroyed by 'formal education'."

This is not the opinion of a few uninformed or disenchanted malcontents. It is also the opinion of many independent thinking educators and scientists. The Commissioner of Education under President Taft, William Harris, states this to be the actual purpose of our education system when he wrote in his book *The Philosophy of Education* that "Ninety-nine [students] out of a hundred are automata, careful to walk in prescribed paths, careful to follow the prescribed custom. This is not an accident but the result of substantial education, which, scientifically defined, is the subsumption of the individual." Even Albert Einstein recognized this when he opined that, "It is, in fact, nothing short of a miracle that the modern methods of instruction have not yet entirely strangled the holy curiosity of inquiry." Some more recent opinions include that of John Gatto, recipient of New York City's 1990 Teacher of the Year award, when he observed that "schools are intended to produce through the application of formulae, formulaic human beings whose behavior can be predicted and controlled" and a California appellate court that ruled as late as 2008 that a "primary purpose of the educational system is to train schoolchildren in good citizenship, patriotism, and loyalty to the state and nation as a means of protecting the public welfare."

The betterment of the individual has been subjugated to the needs of society and the turning point for education appears to have come in 1940. In *The Lonely Crowd* Riesman notes that since then the education system has consistently moved away from developing educated self-thinking individuals to creating citizens who can relate to others. Conformity, sensitivity, and thinking "correctly" has replaced reading, writing, and arithmetic as its primary focus. This was done for two main reasons. The first was that America's military and corporate expansion required people who would be good soldiers and company men. Self-thinkers need not apply. Secondly it made governing easier if the people were "careful to walk in prescribed paths, careful to follow the prescribed custom." Thus the education system became an indoctronation system that discourages personal achievement, individual thinking, and creativity.

In his book, *The Millionaire Mind*, Dr. Thomas Stanley confirms this is also the opinion of many self-made millionaires. One of the interviews he cites is with a successful business owner. This man, despite not having a college education, has successfully built a multi-million dollar business and was commenting on the college education of some of his employees. After watching them in a real life environment he came to the conclusion that as one progresses through college he or she learns "more and more about less and less." Donald Trump reinforces Dr. Stanley's findings. In his book, *Think Big and Kick Ass*, Donald reflects back on his days at Wharton School of Finance and although he appreciates the education he received he felt that it did not satisfy his thirst for "real-world knowledge". To quench this "thirst" he studied real estate in his spare time and this he believes provided him a more useful and beneficial education.

I did a brief analysis of "Forbes 400 Wealthiest People in America" list for 2008 to see if these people's college education was a significant cause of their success. Since I wanted to focus on self-made individuals I took the top 20 and removed anyone whose fortune or business was inherited. This left 11 individuals who built their fortune through their own efforts. I then researched the level of education each one had obtained before their success. The results were surprising. As you can see the majority of them (64%) have little or no college education and none of them have anything higher than a master's degree.

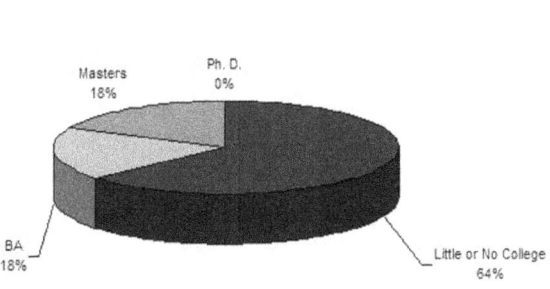

I am not the only one to notice that college is not necessary in order to succeed. *Forbes* came to the same conclusion in a similar investigation. In their study they found that "more than 20% of the 292 of the self-made American billionaires on the most recent list of the World's Billionaires either never started or never completed college." They found the findings so convincing that they titled the April 2, 2009 article *Want to Become a Billionaire? Up Your Chances by Dropping Out of College.*

The next assumption that people make is that these individuals must have had some intellectual advantage that the average person does not have. They must have been gifted in some way, much like natural singers or athletes. But Dr. Stanley's work also debunks this false assumption. While researching *The Millionaire Mind* he discovered that the average self-made millionaire was not in the classes for the gifted nor did they standout as exceptional. They were average students with a modest GPA of 2.9 and an average SAT score of 1100. With an academic record such as this they would be considered "not college material" by most schools.

Dr. Stanley goes on to clarify that he and his subjects are not saying that a college education is not important. Most of the interviewees emphasized the need for a college education to their children. What he and I disagree with is the way it is sold to the public. Conventional wisdom states that a good education and a good career is the best way to financial success. There are two problems with this statement. First is that it is not true and second is that the primary goal of most college students is to get a degree; an education is secondary. Actually getting an education becomes the by-product of getting a degree.

The fact is that the primary reason for a degree is to increase earning potential. In other words a college education is a means to an end and not an end in itself. This is a basic concept that the education system just does not seem to understand. My son John, as a ninth grader, is finishing his first year of high school. Knowing that he really enjoyed and excelled in his Manufacturing Engineering class I asked him if he was planning to choose the "M.E. Academy" as an elective next year.

"I want to" he replied, "but my counselor doesn't want me to because it does not count for college. He wants me to take a performing arts class instead."

While this may seem reasonable to most people, for me it was one of the most illogical things I have ever heard. The "academy" is a special three-year program that offers a select group of students the opportunity to learn the process of designing and manufacturing products. During their time in the class the students will develop skills like drafting, welding, milling and working with CNC machinery. Unlike what is taught in theater arts these are marketable skills that John can use to produce an income to put himself through college. He may even be able to work for himself by doing wrought-iron fencing and repairing corrals. Of course he could take his counselors advice and, like all the other unskilled high school graduates, flip burgers for minimum wage. What does it matter if he goes into debt while working on his degree? In the end he will have it and then be able to make real money!

It is this "college is the only way" thinking that drives so many people into debt for a degree that often does not live up to expectations. Recently I was having a conversation with a tax client and she was telling me about a friend of hers. This friend, after six years and almost $100,000 in student loans, had just graduated with a degree in education and is finally getting her teaching credential. According to Monster.com the average annual salary for a teacher in Riverside County, CA is $52,672 while the starting pay is approximately $45,000. This looks pretty good until one realizes how little difference financially all that sacrifice of time and money makes. Two jobs where a degree is desired but not required is retail and restaurant management. While they may not be as prestigious as being a teacher their pay is equivalent with an average annual income of $52,226 and $55,031 respectively. The main difference is that one does not need to go into debt to pay for the chance to work in those fields. In fact the people who do work in those occupations were paid while they were getting their education.

There is nothing wrong with being a teacher. It is a calling that many have and they do so out of the desire to make a difference in the lives of their students and maybe the world. But others become teachers because it is a "good" or "decent" career. Either way it should be realized that there is a heavy price to pay in time and money before one can teach and the financial rewards do not always live up to expectations. Therefore it needs to be a true passion for those who pursue it. Otherwise they become bitter teachers biding their time until they can retire. This makes them useless to their student and society as a whole.

Robert Kiyosaki's *Success Stories* offers further evidence. In that book a woman tells the story of how she went to school to become a very successful pediatric doctor but still remained ignorant of the knowledge needed to obtain financial independence. As a result she considered herself very intelligent and educated but no matter what she did she and her professional husband never seemed to get ahead financially. As she puts it, "They stuck on the onramp to the financial superhighway." This changed when she volunteered at a local charity and met a couple that were not very "educated" or very intelligent but were very wealthy. At first she was resentful of these people. Here she was and educated professional still struggling financially while these "uneducated" people were living a life of comfort.

The reason for this was that by unquestioningly trusting the understanding of her parents, teachers, and society she put her faith in the conventional wisdom that:

Good Education (Degree)+ Good Career = Financial Success

It was only after she got past the jealousy and opened her mind was she able to see the truth.

Working for Money + Money Working for You = Financial Success

It should be noticed that a degree is not mentioned anywhere in the second formula. This does not mean that earning a degree is a waste of time. What it does mean is that a degree is not a requirement; nor the sole determinant to someone's success. There are alternatives that offer just as much opportunity to succeed in life than getting a college degree and joining the corporate workforce. This is the point that my dad was trying to make so many years ago. That if I wanted to have control over my life and succeed on my terms then I would need to seek alternative ways of educating myself. He was warning me not to fall into the degree trap that tells us that a degree is the panacea of all our financial problems. Instead he wanted me to take classes such as finance, accounting, property management, construction estimating, and surveying. He believed these are classes that would be advantages to running a business and investing in real estate.

My dad still believed in education but it has to be the right education. In his opinion our formal education system is flawed because it perpetuates two myths. The first myth is that the school system was developed to provide an individual the education they need to succeed in life. In reality, as he saw it, the purpose of the school system is to create a needed pool of educated labor that is required to keep an industrialized and technology based society prosperous. This is the reason that our education system, from the first day of kindergarten through the last day of university study, teaches us almost exclusively to work for money. It focuses on teaching us to be good worker bees by conforming and having the skills to perform well as an employee.

Second myth is what I refer to above as the degree trap. The mistaken belief of this myth is that a degree is not only the key to success but is necessary if one is to be a success. As I have shown in the preceding pages there are plenty of non-degreed people who are living proof that the second part of the myth is very questionable and there are two very dangerous and harmful consequences of this myth. The first is that a degree is thought to be an end in itself and, unfortunately for too many, once earned no further education is required. This is highlighted in a story I heard many years ago. A dean of a university was walking around the graduates as they prepared for their commencement ceremony. As he passed a couple of students he was saddened to hear one say, "Thank God this is over with. I am never going to open another book as long as I live."

The second consequence results from the "stated/implied" aspect of everything that is said. By

> College isn't the place to go for ideas.
>
> –Helen Keller (1880-1968)

stating that a degree is an essential key to success we are implying that success is impossible, or nearly impossible, without one. This myth can negatively impact the lives of those who, for whatever reason, do not obtain a college education. Society as a whole views them as being disadvantaged and less capable than their college educated peers.

More importantly, by believing the myth, they believe that they have missed the opportunity to "be someone." They accept the "fact" that the probability of their success is greatly reduced by not getting a college education or degree. As a result they see limitations on their potential and they doubt as to what they can accomplish in life. Many just give up and disappear into the mass of "uneducated workers" and the "disadvantaged" to wait out what remains of their lives. Their only hope being that somebody does something to alleviate their suffering.

> While formal schooling is an important advantage, it is not a guarantee of success nor is its absence a fatal handicap. -Ray Kroc (1902-1984)

I am aware of all the statistics that show that college graduates make more money than non-college graduates and I accept this as fact. What I question is the conclusions that are drawn from these statistics for they do not adequately explain the cause for this disparity in income. It is commonly assumed that since college graduates have extra education it is this education that allows them to make more money. But I have to wonder if it is not the result of people without degrees lowering their expectations because for as long as they can remember they were told by parents, teachers, and society that without a college education that they will never amount to much. If this is so then we are, with the best of intentions, sentencing tens of thousands of young people to a life of helplessness and despair.

Working for Money + Money Working for You = Financial Success

Now that we have an understanding the true formula to financial success it is important to note how this knowledge (or lack of) impacts the lives of Believers and Doubters. First of all Believers realize this is the true way to succeed in life. Second they recognize that both of these components are not equal and concentrate their efforts on the more critical component of having money work for them.

Believers Strategy	
Working for Money	25%
Money Working	75%
Total Effort	100%

Doubters, mostly through lack of knowledge and understanding, base their success on the false formula and put into practice a strategy that all but insures their financial dependence on others.

The Practice of Doubters	
Working for Money	90%
Money Working	10%
Total Effort	100%

As you can see, of the two parts that make up financial success Believers give more importance to having money work for them while Doubters put most of their time and effort into working for money. Dr. Thomas Stanley's research discovered that most self-made millionaires would choose a class that improves their ability to invest their money over a class that will improve their careers. This is because they understand the principles of control and leverage.

Friedrich Hayak, a Nobel Prize winner and "preeminent economist of the last half of the 20th century," wrote in his acclaimed book, *The Road to Serfdom* (1944), that "Economic control is the control of the means to all our ends." He understood that whoever controls our economic lives also has control over all aspects of our lives. He understood that a government that has economic control over the lives of its citizens has just as much power as the most repressive totalitarian state. For Believers this is a basic truth and it applies to employers as well as governments. They understand that while depending on your employer or the government may make you feel "safe" you are trading away your freedom for that "safety" and this includes the freedom to prosper.

To avoid being on the road to serfdom Believers know that they must have money working for them. By focusing on working for money you are not only dependent on others but also limited by the laws of time and space. The fact is that you can only be at one place at any given moment. But having money work for you is a more efficient, productive, and liberating method since money that is hard at work is immune to these laws. It can work in multiple ways and, in some cases, can work 24/7which is beyond the endurance of the human body. This is leveraging.

To help people get a better understanding of this, and keeping with the education theme, I ask my clients to imagine they are taking a hypothetical class called Financial Independence 101. It is the first day of class and they are seated at their desk when they are handed the syllabus outlining the class. Under the grading scale is the breakdown of what makes up the grade each student earns. It has two parts:

Working for Money…………………………………..25%
Money Working for You……………..…… …………75%

I then ask, "With this knowledge, if you wanted to get a good grade in the class where would you place most of your time and effort?"

The obvious answer is having money work for you since concentrating exclusively on working for money can get you an A in that section but you will still get an F for the class. On the other hand by getting a solid A or B in the second section all but insures a good grade in the whole class. Even just getting a decent grade, like a C, in the second section would make it a lot easier to pass the class.

Like all teachers I want you to succeed in this class and in the next chapter I will be covering some of the resources that are available to you. These resources are great starting places but beforehand you must remember a couple of things. First, you must get the right mindset before you can use the tools. Think of a surgeon who is not mentally ready to enter the operating room, much less make the required cuts. What good is the scalpel in his hands? Secondly, unlike the myth that says the only way to succeed is with a degree, the true road to freedom has many paths and it is your duty to find the one that works best for you.

CHAPTER ELEVEN
Non-traditional Education

Learning is not attained by chance,
it must be sought for with ardor
and attended to with diligence.
                              -Abigail Adams (1744-1818)

Since our traditional school system provides a limited and narrow education you will need to look at alternative sources. Although this will require you to dedicate yourself to a lifetime of learning it is essential. In his book "Secrets of the Millionaire Mind" T. Harv Eker writes about the pursuit of education and that those who become rich (financially independent) are constantly learning and growing while poor people (financially dependent) think they already know everything and there is nothing new or useful for them to learn. The famous student of success Earl Nightingale found that the common dominator in the homes of all successful people is a library. By this he does not mean a physical library but that they all had reading material, mostly books. On this realization he began to notice the lack of reading material in the homes of unsuccessful people and drew the conclusion that reading plays a critical role in determining one's development and success.

This is the exact conclusion that David Riesman came to. In *The Lonely Crowd* he details that reading is one of the primary factors in people becoming inner-driven. By studying the history of great historical personalities they often develop an image or ideal that they strive to and that guides them. Additionally, by exploring various topics inner-directed people develop a sense of self-awareness that their other-directed non-reading counterparts never achieve. Finally, by reading several books on the same topic inner-directed individuals learn how to examine several points of view and then come to their own conclusions. This is something that television, no matter how educational, just cannot do.

So the best place to start your alternative education is at your local bookstore. There are volumes upon volumes to choose from. In fact it may be overwhelming and difficult to know where to start. I firmly believe that you have to get the mindset or philosophy of a Believer before you can start using the tools effectively so I suggest that you start with those types of books. In this and previous chapters I have referenced the works of several authors and have included a list in the back of the book to help you start furthering your education. I also recommend that you begin your journey of self-awareness by examining books on several topics. This may help you to uncover some of your hidden talents as you discover a new passion.

> All men who have turned out worth anything have had the chief hand in their own education
> -Sir Walter Scott (1771-1832)

Most of these books are also available on tape and CD. This is an excellent way to learn if you do not have the time to set down and read. These can be played while you are exercising or doing other activities that do not require much mental concentration. Motivational speaker Zig Ziglar recommends a practice that he calls "Automobile U." He points out that many of us pass hours commuting or running errands in our cars. His suggestion is to take the opportunity to learn something that will add value to your life by listening to books on tape or CD. I cannot think of a better way of taking unproductive down time that you are forced to endure and turning it into something that will help you grow and develop as an intelligent independent thinking human being.

Along the same lines as books of CDs or tapes are audio programs on CDs. These usually come in sets of multiple discs with each disc being an in-depth chapter on the subject. As I wrote in the first chapter my dad had me listen to programs such as *I Dare You, The Richest Man in Babylon,* and *Acres of Diamonds* that were similar to the CDs of today but only on vinyl. Although at the time I did not get the implications of what was being taught they did leave an indelible impression on my psyche and helped shape my personality. This is how I prefer to use them. Rather than treating them as a step-by-step process I take a more philosophical approach. By doing so I avoid taking what the presenter says as gospel and it forces me to think about what is being taught. This has two very important benefits. The first is that it develops my analytical and thinking skills. As these develop I rely less and less on the opinions others and gain more and more trust in my own cognitive abilities. This does not mean that I do not listen to expert advice. What it does mean it that I no longer take opinions at face value just because it comes from the mouth of an expert.

Secondly, by mulling it over in my head it makes an impression, either positive or negative, that becomes like a seed that gets me thinking. The seed planted by the positive impression feeds my enthusiasm to learn more and in time grows into a tree of knowledge or expertise. The negative impression also gives me food for thought but only to the extent of why it would not work for me. Either way they sharpen my analytical skills and that is just a valuable as the knowledge I gain.

Note: refer to the Resource section at the end of the book for a recommended list of title and where they can be purchased.

The internet is another good source of knowledge. There are hundreds of websites that offer advice on a multitude of subjects ranging from investing to personal development. Whether they are free or charge a fee I recommend that you treat all websites equally. Consider what they say as suspect until you are knowledgeable enough to discern the good from the bad. With that said they can be good sources to start with and help guide further learning by sparking an interest in one topic or another. Remember that learning that a piece of advice is worthless or just not right for you is learning and should never be considered a waste of time or a lost cause.

For many nothing can compete to a live person being there to teach you and here you have various methods that range in cost and effectiveness. In both Robert Kiyosaki and Donald Trump's books they stress the benefits of seminars. I also agree with them but you will need to be careful since most seminars are nothing more than infomercials for the product or service they are representing. This does not mean that they are not useful. I have been to many of them and I have found them to be very informative.

Being someone whose preferred method of learning is reading I will usually go to a seminar with the hope that they will recommend a few books that will help me gain a better understanding of the subject. In this way I can do some inexpensive learning before I decide if the topic is something I wish to pursue or not. During many of these seminars the speaker usually tries to educate the audience as best he or she can during the allotted time. As a result you may get enough information to get your education started. This may even answer the question if this is the way you want to go. Many times I have attended seminars that talked on a subject that I thought would be interesting only to find the opposite to be true. I have never considered these to be a waste of time since learning something is still learning. No matter what I learn I am better off for having gone to them.

> What we become depends on what we read after all of the professors have finished with us. The greatest university of all is a collection of books.
> -Thomas Carlyle (1795-1881)

The ones I have been to that I think were a waste of time were the seminars that were all sales and had zero educational value. Some were giving the attendees such a hard sell that I left halfway through. Being in sales most of my life I have always felt that the product should speak for itself and the more you need to pressure someone to buy the less value they are getting for their money. This is not to say that these programs are not beneficial. Many of them are but with price tags that range from a few hundred to a few thousand dollars you will need to be careful in choosing the right one.

Obviously you want to get the most education for you dollar and I believe that I found the best way to do this. I recommend that you attend the introductory infomercial and get as mush information on the subject as possible. If it looks like something you would be interested in doing then go out and get some books on the subject. Again the speaker may list a few titles in the seminar. If not you will get some terms that will allow you to do a search at amazon.com. I find the reviews of other readers very helpful and will try to read all of them if possible. If there are too many then I'll pick some samples from the excellent, so-so, and do not buy categories. Either way you will want to read the good and bad comments before buying any books. Only after reading several books on the subject should you register for one of these programs. The last thing you want to do is pay the tuition of a university for an elementary school level education.

I was fortunate enough to have my father to help but when he passed away in 2004 I was left without his guidance. The real estate market in California was reaching a fever pitch and the ability to get an investment property that would cash flow was next to impossible so I decided to go out-of-state. Since my dad stayed within California to invest I had no knowledge of what it took or even how to start looking for property in other states. I started buying and reading books on the subject but I still felt that I did not have the knowledge to confidently go out and invest. So in October of 2006 I signed up for the Real Estate Mentoring program at Trump University. I was matched up with a great mentor who was a retired commercial real estate broker with over thirty years of investment experience.

Since I had already gained so much knowledge before hand we were able to get right into the more advance principles of investing in not only out-of-state properties but in multifamily and commercial properties also. Over the year that I was in the program I learned to research markets and the how to evaluate the individual properties. This helped me focus my search on the most promising markets and the best properties.

Unfortunately, by the time I was knowledgeable enough to benefit from the program California's real estate market began to collapse and I was no longer financially able to do so. Not to be one who gives up easily I was able to put together an investment package for several California investors to buy in Idaho. These initial transactions not only paid me back the initial investment I made in the education; it tripled it. I am also confident that when the economy recovers I will be able to use this knowledge to get an even greater return.

They say that people love to talk about themselves and I found this to be 100% true. In Robert Kiyosaki's book *Retire Rich, Retire Young* he recounts a conversation he had with a very successful and wealthy businessman. This gentleman was lamenting the fact that "his family asks for money, his employees asks for raises, but nobody asks for his advice". This is how I received a lot of my knowledge. I found by asking pointed question you can gain some of the most valuable lessons on life for little or no money.

From these "been there, done that" individuals I was able to get real-world knowledge that is impossible to receive from a book. This is why I always preferred part-time instructors in college. In my Multinational Marketing class the part-time instructor was the owner of a company that was heavily involved in international trade. After we would cover a chapter of the textbook he would always finish with, "I know the book says this but in the real world it is like…"

Most successful people are proud of their accomplishments and are happy to share their knowledge with you. If you are sincere and truly desire to learn from them you are not bothering them, you are paying them the greatest compliment that one can receive. Remember you are the student and they are the teachers. All you have to do is to be willing to listen and learn. Do not be afraid to ask pointed direct questions when you need a better understanding of the subject. Remember that they were once just as unknowledgeable as you are now and they will respect your honesty.

I cannot overestimate how powerful a tool this is to your success. The author David Nasaw writes in his best-selling biography of Andrew Carnegie that this is how the now legendary icon of American capitalism got his start. With his father only managing to work as a part-time weaver young Andrew had no one to teach him about money and business. Refusing to consider himself disadvantaged he sought out those who could teach him how to succeed. He asked his bosses and other successful people their advice. As he got older he and a few of his friends formed an unofficial club. Since there was no television to waste time on they started meeting for the sole purpose of having something to do. In time business and investing became a favorite topic and soon became the focal point of the meetings. In time they became each other's teachers and I find that it is very interesting that every member of that group regardless of their formal education or where they started in life ended it as very successful and prosperous men.

This illustrates that it is a two-way relationship since each member learned from each other. This is very important because you cannot be seen as being phony or just after other people's knowledge. The best teacher you can have is one who cares about your success but you will need to reciprocate by doing what you can for them. You need to understand that we all have

> No man is your enemy, no man is your friend, every man is your teacher
> ~ Anonymous

knowledge and abilities that others do not have so do not undervalue what you have to offer.

You need to recognize that it is very difficult to find people who want to make something out of their lives and in all likelihood you will not find them among your current set of friends. Therefore you must look outside your comfort zone and reach out to people you would normally not associate with. One option is too find an investment groups that hold regular meetings in your community. In most metropolitan areas there are usually several that are open to anyone who wants to attend. In my area there is one that specializes in real estate investing and has monthly meetings. These meeting have experts in the field come and share their knowledge with the attendees. They also provide social time where attendees can get to know each other. I highly recommend finding a group like this in your area since it allows you to increase your education and develop relationships with like-minded people. Again, avoid anyone trying to sell you something until you have enough confidence in your knowledge to make an educated decision.

Be mindful that the main reason why most of us never find our teachers is because our insecurities block us from seeing them. Jealousy, envy, contempt, arrogance, fear and other unhelpful feelings prevent us from being able to develop mutually beneficial relationships with

> Anyone who stops learning is old, whether at twenty or eighty. Anyone who keeps learning stays young. The greatest thing in life is to keep your mind young.
>
> ~ Henry Ford (1863-1947)

Believers & Doubters

those who are different from us. Fear, the destructor of all that is good, is the biggest inhibitor of all. The fear of not being accepted, the fear of looking foolish, the fear of looking stupid or ignorant keeps us from gaining knowledge from others. As a result many of us stay within our comfort zone and associate with people like ourselves. We live in communities made up of similar people who have similar beliefs and knowledge. At work we often surround ourselves with people who do not have anything more to add to our education than we do to theirs and our lives become stagnant as we commute from one unenlightening environment to another.

In time our growth and development ceases and along with them all the possibilities that life holds for us. We stop learning and fall first into a routine and then into a rut. Our natural desire to learn and prosper is dulled by the lack of stimulation and, I believe, we stop living and start dying. Initially it begins with intellectual death that is soon followed by spiritual and emotional death. Physical death is the last and sometimes takes the longest to pass. It is not uncommon for people to be intellectually, spiritually, and emotionally dead for years and even decades before physical death relieves them of their anguish. If you do not want to start dying and do want to keep life full then I recommend that you continue to grow and develop by dedicating yourself to a lifetime of learning.

> Live as if you were to die tomorrow.
> Learn as if you were to live forever.
> - Mahatma Gandhi
> (1869-1948)

Non-traditional Education

Some observations by
General Douglas MacArthur (1880-1964)

People grow old only by deserting their ideals.

Years may wrinkle the skin, but to give up interest wrinkles the soul.

You are as young as your faith, as old as your doubt, as young as your self-confidence, as old as your fear, as young as your hope, as old as your despair

In the place of every heart is a recording chamber; so long as it receives messages of beauty, hope, cheer, and courage, so long are you young. It is when your heart is covered with the snows of pessimism and the ice of cynicism, then and only then are you grown old- and then, indeed, as the ballad say, you just fade away....

Chapter 12
The Most Important Decision

Can you live forever? Marry the wrong spouse and everyday will feel like an eternity. Marry the right spouse and life will be joyful and perhaps even a rich experience.

–Dr. Thomas Stanley

The above quote is from Dr. Thomas Stanley's best-selling book *The Millionaire Mind* where he dedicates 43 pages, over 10% of the book, to a chapter on the importance of choosing the correct spouse. Of course we all know that the selection of whom we will be sharing our life with is one of the biggest decisions one can make in his or her life but what we often do not understand is how important that person is in determining our successes and failures in life. Marry the right person and he or she will be an asset that will help you achieve all that you are capable of and make life worth living. Marry the wrong person and you could find yourself with the proverbial "ball and chain" that holds you back from all the success you are capable of. The self-made millionaires in Dr. Stanley's book demonstrated the importance of understanding this when 81% of the more than 700 interviewed stated that having the right spouse was an important or a very important factor in their success.

As the saying goes 'behind every great man is a great woman" and any in-depth study of great historical figures will find them to have been single (or virtually single), or married to a supportive spouse. Two examples of this are the Churchills and the Adamses. What makes these two marriages so extraordinary is that a large percentage of communication between the spouses was in written form thus creating a written record of the dialog that passed between them. In the Churchills' case it was due to Winston's lack of ability to remember anything that was not written down and for the Adamses it was the long periods of separation in which letters were the sole method of communication.

> My most brilliant achievement was my ability to be able to persuade my wife to marry me.
> - Winston Churchill (1874-1965)

Winston Churchill is most known for leading Great Britain's defiant stand against Hitler's yet undefeated Third Reich. Even in the darkest days, when defeat appeared inevitable, Churchill would take to the airwaves with a bombastic oratory that filled the British people with hope and optimism. What many people do not realize was that in private he was susceptible to bouts of depression that he called his "black dog days" and that for the ten years preceding him becoming prime minister his political career was considered all but over. When he spoke in parliament the halls, once filled with people who used to line up to hear him, were often nearly empty. Winston himself began to doubt if he would ever return to power and fulfill "his destiny" and on several occasions became despondent.

Clementine Churchill knew better. Having just as much internal fortitude she was able to do for Winston what he did for his country: to give the inspiration to persevere even though all seemed lost. Just as he believed and had faith in the people of his "island nation" she believed in the man she married. Not even in 1930s, during those the dark days when Winston was considered to be in the "waning days" of his political life, would Clementine allow the cynical comments of the wives of the other powerful men of the time to convince her that her husband was not destined for greatness. This faith in him allowed her to support and inspire Winston through those dark days of despair. She used it to keep him motivated and he came to depend on her. The man who would become known as the "Greatest Statesman of the 20th Century" was the first to say that he would not have been able to do it if it was not for the support, love, and faith of his wife Clementine.

Unlike Winston Churchill, John Adams did not consider himself to be a great man. Although he was highly intelligent he never felt that he was destined to be anything other than a competent attorney in colonial Boston. Events dictated otherwise and John soon found himself first in the service of Massachusetts as a delegate to the Continental Congress and then to the young nation of the United States as ambassador to France followed by Great Britain. Upon his return from Europe he became Vice-president to George Washington, and finally ended his career by succeeding Washington and becoming the second President of the United States. He was instrumental in the founding of this country by being a passionate advocate for independence and helped the

United States gain recognition by the other European powers, thus insuring American independence.

Supporting him through it all was his wife Abigail. This took great courage for if they found themselves on the losing end of the conflict John would have been hanged thus leaving Abigail and their three children financially destitute. But it was not courage that set Abigail apart for many women of the time faced the same consequences. What is unique about Abigail Adams was that not only did she courageously believe in her husband but that she was also his intellectual equal. John would often use her as a sounding board for his ideas and arguments. Being a highly intelligent man he often did not have the understanding or sensitivity that many legal and political situations required. His quick wit and equally sharp tongue would often alienate people whose support he desperately needed. Abigail became a moderating force that allowed John to play a more effective role in the congress by helping him to avoid getting carried away by his own passions.

Those who supported John Adams in the congress soon recognized the role Abigail played and rather then be disturbed by it did everything in their power to assist her. General Washington arranged so that his personal courier would carry Abigail's correspondence from Boston to John in Philadelphia thus insuring that John would receive all of Abigail's wise counsel. There was no doubt in the minds of his supporters that John would not be as good as he was if it were not for Abigail. They came to respect her intelligence to such a degree that when the chance permitted they would seek her out for advice and guidance. George Washington and Thomas Jefferson are just two of the "great men" who became in awed by this Boston Attorney's wise and intelligent wife. After Abigail's passing John Adams would often comment that it was she who was his most important advisor and who gave him his best advise.

These are just two examples of how being married to the right person can determine one's success in life. Neither Winston nor John would be the great men that they became if it were not for the women they married. This makes perfect sense once we understand the affect people have on us. I have read the books of several teachers of success and they all say the same thing: positive people help and negative people hurt. The fact is that people can motivate and inspire us or they can demoralize us. It is also true that an ounce of negative energy can overcome a pound of positive energy. Doubt and fear become like illnesses that can spread from one person to another leaving their victims demoralized and psychologically incapacitated. This is why it is easier to make the brave scared than it is to make the scared brave.

Even in the most casual or impersonal settings the attitude of a negative person can have enormous impact on how we think. In a marriage, which is as personal and intimate relationship one can have, the negative Doubter is fully capable of destroying their spouse's hopes, dreams, and enthusiasm. Being exposed to their pessimistic and fearful attitude on a daily basis can, like water wears on a rock, overcome the positive attitude of even the most strongest and resistant soul. A few years of living in such a toxic atmosphere usually leaves one broken and demoralized. On the other hand having a positive, confident, individual as your souse can help you to overcome obstacles that block the way to your dreams and provide you with the reassurance we all need when facing difficult situations.

This is what the people that Dr. Stanley researched clearly understood when they gave there choice of spouse such importance. Dr. Stanley investigated deeper and found that although physical attributes were factors in their choice of a spouse it was not the most important. When asked to describe what attracted them to their spouses' adjectives such as beauty, pretty, gorgeous, sexy, etc was very seldom used. Instead the Millionaires preferred to use more meaningful words such as intelligent, sincere, cheerful, reliable, and affectionate. By focusing on these attributes they were able to find individuals that were true partners in life and who actively participated in their success.

This approach has also served them well in obtaining marital and well as financial bless. Only 2% were divorced and the average had been married for 28 years. When compared to national averages where more that half of marriages end in divorce it appears that these people understand that the key to a successful and having a fulfilled life is not to just to be a Believer but to also marry one. This is the optimal combination that allowed individuals like Winston Churchill and John Adams to become great historical figures and lead them to have such deep devoted and very successful marriages. Marriages that continuously regenerated their hearts and inspired their spirits.

Doubters can have successful marriages to as long as they are married to other Doubters. If the Believer/Believer combination is not possible then Doubter/Doubter is the next best option. Doubters tend to accept situations as they are and, although they may complain a lot, usually adapt to their "place" in life. This contentment places less demands on them and their spouses since their expectations of and from each other are lower. While it is highly improbable that two Doubters will be able to reach their full potential in life they may be able to create a very loving and caring family life. It is not that difficult to think of people who did not be all that they could be in other parts of their lives but who had a great family life. They were successful husband and wives, fathers and mothers. Their lives were rich in ways financial success alone cannot provide.

The worst marriage situation is when a Believer and a Doubter wed. Usually this combination reduces the potential that the Believer had in life. Only the strongest of Believers, without the support and under the constant pessimism and fear of the Doubting spouse, are able to achieve their full potential. In most cases the doubting spouse becomes like the figurative 'ball and chain' that restricts the movement, and potential, of the other spouse. What is worse is that the Doubter's other-directedness makes them inconsistent and their fragile self-confidence prevents them from attempting any form of introspection. Thus they usually never see that their attitudes are the cause of their family's lack of success. This only makes them more hostile to their spouses and generates a negatively charged environment within the home.

This situation usually ends in one of two ways. Initially the Believer will try to bring the Doubter on his or her journey of growth, learning, and improvement. If they are successful then they will be able inspire or motivate the Doubter into becoming a more positive, optimistic, and self-confident individual. This is the best result that one can hope for but with the Doubter's avoidance to change it is the least probable. What usually results is the Believer becoming frustrated at the Doubter's lack of desire to improve, learn and grow. This is something most Believers cannot comprehend since they see our ability to do these things as distinctly human and to not do so is to reduce us to the level of a basic animal. In response the Doubter is resentful of being pushed into doing something that he or she is resistant to doing. The Doubter will see the Believer's actions as either an attempt to control or implying that the Doubter is somehow flawed or requires improvement.

In the end many Believers will take the journey alone. They will no longer be satisfied with life "as is" and will seek out ways to improve it. They will desire companions who will not only provide the support that their spouses do not provide but who also stimulates their need to become a better and more developed person. Over time they will develop and outgrow the more stationary spouse. This means that although they may have been at the same level of growth and development at the time they met they have now "grown apart." The result is after several or more years a broken marriage and divorce.

For many people, even Believers, taking a life-changing journey alone is almost impossible. This is especially true of a journey that requires one to enter into the unknown of his or her future. The chances of success in this type of endeavor are further reduced by having a non-supporting spouse that weighs one down rather than lift them up. Very few have the strength to resist the corrosive effects of the spouse's negative influences. As a result their spirit dies a little each day until all that remains is a broken Believer. Being a broken Believer is worse than being a Doubter. Doubters are content with their situation but broken Believers hate where they are in life and desire to do more. Only now they no longer have the will to resist. In many ways they are like a stallion that was once a big and powerful beast but, as a result of daily abuse, is now a broken-spirited domestic animal whose sole purpose in life is serving their master. Life truly becomes a purgatory and many are freed only at the end of their lives.

This is why it is imperative that we understand the role our spouses play in our lives and why it is important to choose wisely. For the single readers I recommend that you learn from the examples set by Dr. Stanley's subjects. You will want to look deeper into what a prospective mate will do to your life and what you are going to do to that person's life. Are they going to be an asset in your life? Are you going to be one in theirs? Are they bringing their best self into the relationship or are they looking for someone to do that for them? Are you bringing your best self? Are you adding to someone's life or are you looking for someone to add to yours?

If you are a Believer than you will want another Believer at your side. Life is already difficult enough without having someone you cannot count on or does not have the capability to handle its ups and downs. This may be difficult since men are naturally drawn to "damsels in distress" and women's natural desire to nurture leads them to be attracted to males in need of care. In the end what they usually get are distressed damsels and damaged males. I recommend that you leave the distressed damsels and the damaged men to find each other and that you find a mentally and emotionally healthy partner for your life.

If you are a Doubter then do not marry a Believer. Remember that your potential is inside of you and not someone else. Only you can unleash it through personal growth and development. A Believer cannot do this for you nor can he or she remove the fear and uncertainty you have. To think otherwise is wholly unrealistic and unfair to the Believer. If you decide to try and grow as a Believer then wait until you are well developed and comfortable with where you are on your journey before taking a life partner. Otherwise marry a fellow Doubter. In the end your life will be more pleasant and you will not be reducing another person's chances at happiness. This is even more imperative if you love that person because you will be doing this out of love for them. To

Most Important Decision

do anything different would be selfish and cruel since you will be sentencing the Believer to a prison term that can only end in heartache. Your belief systems will never be reconciled. The differences will only get bigger over time. So trust me when I say this can only end in misery for the both of you and the cost is too great of a price to pay, especially if children become involved.

The chances are that you are already married. If this is the case then things can be a bit more complicated. You may or may not be a Believer and your spouse may be or may not be a Doubter. If you are reading this book you are probably a Believer or a Doubter willing to become a Believer. If this is the case then you need to establish the mindset of your spouse and the easiest why to do this is to ask them to read this book or one similar to it. If he or she is willing to do so or at least willing to discuss what you have learned then there is a very good chance that you will be able to move forward together. If they are not willing to read the book then you have a very good indication that he or she is a Doubter who is unwilling to change.

A situation like this can create a dilemma that can have dire consequences for you and your marriage. There are two options that are open and each has its own risk and reward. The first option is to proceed on your journey of self-enrichment and self-development alone. In his book *The Millionaire Mindset* T. Harv Eker offers this as the preferred manner in which to move forward. If done correctly you may set an example by which your spouse can become motivated by your example and join you on your quest. While this is a worthy and ideal situation to strive for it does have numerous obstacles, which you do not have the power to overcome. We need to always remember that we can have the power to influence people, but we do not have the capability to control them. Your success will be based on whether or not your spouse is willing to be open to your influences. The other problem is that you will have some setbacks on your journey and your spouse will need to be strong enough to overcome their fears in order to continue in the journey. Otherwise he or she is liable to turn tail at the slightest setback and return to his or her comfort zone. Of course in their mind you are the one responsible for these setback and you will probably pay an emotional price for your foolishness. As a result you may find that you have reached your full potential but lost your marriage in the process.

As I stated above, two Doubters can go on to live wonderful and fulfilling lives together. They may never make their mark on the world or have the all the success they are capable of but they are rich none-the-less. This is not a bad thing and many have happily made the choice to dedicate their lives to achieving success in this noble endeavor. But it does require great sacrifice and you must be willing to settle for being a successful leader of a family. It also has its own share of risk. The biggest difficulty you will face is that your success is dependent on the cooperation of your spouse. It is important to remember that two Doubters make the best couple in this situation since their expectations of each other are low. If your spouse married you because he or she saw that you had the ability to change his or her life in a way that they are unwilling or unable to do for themselves then they will not be satisfied with your lack of achievement and, always looking for external causes for their own dissatisfaction, will blame you for not meeting your full potential. They will not appreciate the sacrifice you are making and resentment will grow on all sides. This is a losing situation that most Believers cannot overcome and is deadly to any marriage.

If you do decide to choose your marriage over all else then I must strongly recommend that you stop your journey of self-improvement and growth right here. Every word you read about being a Believer will forever alter your way of thinking and only increase your thirst for something more in life. Do not read another book, page, paragraph or sentence for in this case ignorance is truly blessed. Be content with who you are and live your life with the satisfaction that you made one of the greatest sacrifices that a person can make for his or her family: the sacrifice of self-fulfillment. There is no shame in this and it is a decision that deserves respect. Just make sure your family, especially your spouse, appreciates it otherwise it will be a sacrifice made in vain.

There are also no guarantees that a marriage between two Believers will be successful either. One of the most common problems I see in these marriages is that each spouse is pursuing separate agendas with common effort being limited to the sphere of the family. A good example of this is that many couples cannot even get on the same page when it comes to money and it is not uncommon for each to have individual checking accounts for "their" money. This may seem to be a reasonable approach to take since each spouse is making his or her "own" money but it destroys the benefit of any synergy that the couple may have. Synergy basically means that the whole is greater than the sum of its parts or, simplistically, that 1 plus 1 is equal to 3. In other words two people working together can accomplish just as mush as three or more working separately. This is something that great marriages achieve and it is why the Churchills and the Adamses were able to accomplish so much. Unfortunately this is something that most couple fails to recognize and they end up making their lives a lot harder and stressful than it needs to be by directing their efforts in different, or even opposite, directions of each other.

As an aid I recommend that the couple do the Vision Statement exercise in chapter seven and create a vision for the marriage and family. What is important is that both spouses are equals in creating the statement. It should reflect the wants and needs of all members of the family and offers each one the ability to reach their potential while staying within the framework of the family. This may require some negotiating and sacrifice by both spouses and do not be discouraged if it takes several tries to get it right. Remember, it took several years to come up with the final draft of the Constitution and that your statement, like that great document, should be designed to guide you through life, not dictate it. If properly done and correctly applied you and your spouse will see a marked improvement in all aspects of your lives. The synergy created will translate into less stress and more time for living. Life may even become a joyful and perhaps even an enriching experience

Two are better than one, because they have a good return for their work:

If one falls down, his friend can help him up. But pity the man who falls and has no one to help him up!

Also, if two lie down together, they will keep warm. But how can one keep warm alone?

Though one may be overpowered, two can defend themselves. A cord of three strands is not quickly broken.

Ecclesiastes 4

CHAPTER THIRTEEN
What About the Children

A child educated only at school is an uneducated child.
George Santayana (1863-1952)

Whether it is over a client's kitchen table or during a presentation I am often asked by concerned parents what can they do differently that will give their children a better chance to succeed in the world. I will say here that I am not an expert on raising children but after being raised the way that I was, which was out of the norm for my generation, and spending a lifetime studying others I have come to understand the one factor that truly determines whether we have lives that are meaningful and worth living or not. This factor is the ability to discover one's natural talents and his or her "calling" or purpose in life. I strongly believe that all humans have this within them and the only way to happiness and success is by discovering it. While school, athletics, and other youth programs can help they are of no use if the child's home does not provide an atmosphere that allows the child to discover the potential within. This means that the parents play key roles in helping their children and in this chapter I will highlight three areas were parents, contrary to their best intentions, are actually hampering this process and restricting their children's ability to discover their purposes in life.

Myth #1
A parent's prime responsibility is to protect their children

While I do believe that protecting our children should be a priority in our lives I fundamentally disagree that it should take precedence over everything else. What I believe is more important than protecting my children and getting them into adulthood alive is to prepare them to become independent adults capable of providing for themselves. In order to do so I must create an atmosphere that allows my children to discover their natural talents, passions, and life's purpose. This often requires that I put their physical safety second so that they can grow emotionally, intellectually, and psychologically. Only by controlling my instinctive impulse to protect can they develop the confidence needed to be a Believer and to reach their full potential.

The problem is that in today's society protectionism is not only unrestrained it is running rampant. Not only are parents striving to protect their children from hurt bodies but also from hurt feelings. It appears now that children are no longer permitted to feel anything but joyful and happy emotions. Anything that creates discomfort, fear, anxiety, or sorrow is to be avoided at all cost. To do otherwise is to damage the child's fragile psyche and cripple him or her for life. So now all players, regardless of ability, are trophy-winning athletes. Every team, whether they won or lost all their games, are champions. And in some cases they can even graduate from high school without ever having learned the ability to read or do basic math. I guess feeling good is more important in life than being literate and when it comes to feeling good no child is to be left behind.

This is where protectionism does more harm than good. Not only for the obvious reason that it leaves the child completely emotionally unprepared for the realities of life but it also retards their development and denies them the opportunities to discover their natural abilities. As a result they never get to know what their purpose is in life and often suffer from a sense of being "lost" in life. This can have far reaching consequences since people who have a sense of purpose in their lives are more likely to be successful and happy while the "lost" souls are more likely to suffer from depression and resort to drug and alcohol abuse. Having a purpose in life does more to positively motivate a person than the groundless ego boosting ever can.

In 500 B.C. the great Chinese philosopher Sun Tzu wrote the axiom that "you must reinforce success and starve failure." Unfortunately only way to discover a child's natural abilities and to uncover where he or she will succeed in life is for the child to go through process of trial and error. This requires the parents to step back and allow the child to fail. This is the only way that the child can discover what he is and is not good at. This is not a bad event in a child's life and if handled correctly can be a very good experience for him of her. From these experiences children have the opportunity to learn that they cannot be good at everything. Rather than protect them from this truth it should be explained to them that some kids are naturally better at some things while they are naturally better at other things. That we all have our talents and abilities and that these strengths and weaknesses do not make us better or worse then anyone else. This is why we must depend on each other. Even the greatest and most gifted athletes, artists, and musicians cannot go it alone. They often need people with different abilities to help keep them successful.

This is a more effective method than empty ego boosting because it is based in reality and does not underestimate the child's intelligence. A child knows when they are bad at something or when something is not for them. No amount of parent enthusiasm and motivation can convince a child otherwise. In most cases the parent is just insulting the child's intelligence and forcing the child to feel that he or she is not living up to expectations. So instead of instilling confidence the parent destroys it and loses credibility with the child. On the other hand by being honest and forthright in a positive and supportive manner the child will come to see the parent as an honest and straight talking person who will tell them what they need to hear. This creates an environment where the parent can play an important role in helping the child grow into adulthood rather than being reduced to a parent that only offers empty platitudes and false hopes.

Unfortunately many parents do just the opposite with the unrealistic approach that tries to convince the child that he or she has the ability to do everything well. In most cases they end up reinforcing failure by directing the child's time and energy, not to mention family resources, into activities that he or she has little chance of gaining success in. As a result the child's confidence is lowed rather than increased and a Doubter's mindset begins to develop. More importantly it usually keeps hidden the areas of true potential that lie within the child and an opportunity to provide him with a positive self-image is forever lost.

1. If your child has a passion support it with all your ability. By doing so you will be supporting success and avoiding needless failure.

2. If your child has not found their passion encourage them to explore as many subjects,

activities, etc as possible. You never know what might "turn them on."

3. Recognize the difference between a failure and a setback. For our purposes here a failure is when a child is attempting to do something that he or she does not have the natural ability that will lead to success. A setback is what happens when the child has the ability but things did not come out as planned or as wished for. Setbacks provide the opportunity to learn, develop, and to become stronger.

4. Be honest with yourself. You know when something is not working for your child and is a failure. If the child is not progressing in an activity, as he or she should be. then you might need to find something else for the child to do. This is were #2 is very important and requires you to access your child's abilities and chances to succeed in a very objective manner.

5. Remember that children do things for fun. Your child may play a sport that they have basic competency in just because they like it and are having fun. If this is the case let them enjoy themselves and leave the criticism to the parents' of the "superstars."

6. Try to recognize if they are doing this for them or to please you. In an attempt to please parents and stay connected to them many children will try to pursue their parents' passions. You need to let your children know that it is perfectly OK for them to pursue their

own interest and if it is the same as the parents', great. If not, that is OK too.

7. This is their life. Just because you would not enjoy what they are doing does not mean that it is not rewarding and satisfying to them. They are taking the first steps in discovering THEIR purpose in life and you have no right to impose yours on them.

A note on failure: It is very difficult for parents to recognize that their children do not have the ability to successfully do everything they want. It is even more difficult to tell this to children especially if it is something they really enjoy doing. In many cases you can handle it without mentioning the F word by just introducing a new activity, interest, or hobby. In a few cases you may need explain that not everyone is meant to do everything and, if they wish to continue with the activity, to encourage the child to do be content with doing their best. This will let them work the situation out for themselves. In extreme cases your child will be told that they just are not good enough. This is not a bad thing. I remember when I was in elementary school and all my friends made the school choir. When I tried out I was crushed when the teacher truthfully told me I cannot sing but it was better that she did rather than Simon Cowell scolding me in front of millions on *American Idol*.

Myth #2
Performance in school indicates future performance in life

This is an area where even the most well-intentioned parent does damage to their children. Since my children were young I was involved in many of their activities including being Cub Master for five years and Chairperson for their elementary school Site Council. During those years and the ones that followed I have seen parents and educators put extreme pressure on children to perform well academically. The pride of most parents is to have their child in a class for the "gifted" or other such programs. I have even seen parents demand that their child be put with certain teachers or in certain schools so that their children can get a "good" education.

On the surface this seems like a reasonable attitude for parents to take and I applaud the efforts these parents are making. The problem is that it is based on the faulty assumption that a college degree is a must to succeed in this world and that most, if not all learning, is achieved through formal education. This leads parents to come to the conclusion that the "better" the formal education the "better" their child will do in life. Therefore, parents must do all they can so that their child will have the opportunity to go to a "good" school. This creates a situation where a child's performance in school is mistakenly used to determine the chances of his or her future success. This myth or belief has become so much apart of conventional wisdom that to question it or to propose an alternative would lead many to question one's judgment and fitness to be a parent.

The problem is that this belief is based on another myth; that our education system is designed to provide children with the education they will need to succeed in life. It is good to recall from chapter 7 that as early as 1940 our education system has been steadily moving away from the focus of educating individuals to that of producing conforming and sensitive people who are in tuned with others. In other words, producing people who will "protect the public welfare" by being "good citizens" while providing corporations with a large pool of compliant workers. Thus the primary objective of the schools is, as John Gatto, New York City's 1990 Teacher of the Year states, 'to produce through the application of formulae, formulaic human beings whose behavior can be predicted and controlled." Such a philosophy creates an atmosphere where compliance and sensitivity becomes more important that intelligence and creativity. While this may be good for corporations and the public welfare it is disastrous for the individual and is the primary reason our public schools consistently produce people who are unprepared for life.

Unfortunately most parents accept these myths as facts and encourage their children to blindly walk the same "prescribed paths" and to follow the same "prescribed custom" regardless of the results. Therefore they stress that good grades and a good formal education is the most important factor in being able to achieve success in life. This also infers that, contrarily, by not getting good grades or a good formal education children are forever doomed to a substandard life of mediocrity.

> Imagination is more important than knowledge.
> - Albert Einstein
> (1879-1955)

The truth is that while school performance is important it need not determine the future success of any child. As I explained in the chapter on Alternative Education there is ample evidence that there is no connection between school performance and success in life. There are plenty of people who were at the top of their classes, graduated with honors, and earned degrees from a top-rated university only to end up with mediocre jobs and lifestyles. Conversely there are plenty of average, or even below average, students who went on to become very successful individuals and are contributing more to society than their "gifted" schoolmates (see below).

This has lead many to question the usefulness of programs for the "gifted" in schools. William Manchester, the foremost biographer of Winston Churchill, quotes a University of Chicago study that found that the "Gifted" programs tend to focus on intelligent but non-creative children who are compliant and good test-takers. In other words, they are the type of children that thrive in the Other-directed dominated education system. If truth be told not only would Winston Churchill be considered not "gifted" but so would the likes of Einstein, Mark Twain, Picasso, and Thomas Edison. So do not become too depressed if your child is not considered "gifted" by his or her school. It may be an indication that he has an Inner-directed (Believer) personality and cannot be easily influence by other including teachers. Just remember that he or she is in great company.

Additionally I am not against getting a college education. One of the objectives of this book is the need for continuous life long learning and for many that includes a college education. But the reality is that a university education is not for everyone and not all children will or need to go to college. This does not mean that those who do not go to college are doomed to be failures. As I stated in chapter 10 of the top twenty of Forbes Wealthiest Americans 64% had little or no college education and the majority of the successful individuals studied in the *Millionaire Next Door* were average students who received little if any formal education after high school. I believe the key is that these "undereducated" individuals found their purpose in life that allowed them to excel way beyond what their college educated counterparts were able to do. I also think that it is telling that these people have the ability to pay college educated people to work for them.

One of the factors that allow this myth to continue is that many of today's parents are other-directed and were brought up believing what they were told. When it did not perform as promised they decided it was because they did not take their formal education seriously enough. So instead of re-evaluating what they were taught to believe they turn around and, in a misguided attempt, try to help their children from making the same mistake as they did. As a result they are exposing their children to the same falsehood that lead to their own lack of success in life. In turn, this overemphasis on formal education forces the children to judge their own success by how well they are performing in school. For too many they develop the opinion that they are either successful in school or doomed to be losers. The consequences of which is that it prevents children from exploring non-college alternatives and retards their chances of uncovering their hidden purpose and natural talents.

This causes problems for children, especially those who are bright and creative enough to question what they are told. By the time they are in middle school smart kids begin to question wisdom of what they are being taught. They know of people who were "gifted" students only to go on and become embittered by the lack of success in life and others who, without all the accolades and formal education, went on to become very successful people. This is the reality that our young people see and they become skeptic of the dogma being espoused by their parents and educators. This is why I am amused when educated adults who have given up on their dreams and on their own chances of success are shocked when their attempts to motivate academically underachieving children fail. In an attempt to inspire children by telling how important grades are and that a college education is the key to success these adults are really telling children, "I sacrificed in order to get good grades and going to college and look, my life still sucks." Do not underestimate the intelligence of your children; they may see the truth before you do.

This also helps to explain why so many students perform below what they are capable of. It is not because they are lazy. It is because they wisely do not see the benefit. In my opinion, the problem is not how well they are performing in school, but that there are no other alternatives being offered. This forces the non-college going child to accept as fact that they are forever destined to a life of limited opportunities, low ambitions, and unfulfilled dreams. In the end it becomes a self-fulfilling prophecy that has more impact on their lives then their academic performance ever will.

The next question is what should a parent do for their children. Whether they are good or bad students I recommend the following:

1. Accept the fact that not all children will go or need to go to college and that this does not mean that they cannot "make something" of their lives.
2. While stressing that grades, academic achievement, and a college education are important they are not the keys to success that everyone says they are. Stress the fact that the key to success and a fulfilled life is to discover a purpose in life. In this case it is what the child does outside of school that becomes more important than what they do in school. Try to encourage them to explore as many different activities as possible until they find one that they develop a true passion for.

3. Once they find a passion encourage it with as much enthusiasm as you can muster even if you do not believe it is for them. Remember that this is your child's life not yours. If you want to do something different with your life then do it. Do not try to do it through your child.

4. Stress that education does not end with school. Learning is a lifelong endeavor and that the most important lessons are learned outside of school.

5. Encourage at all cost for your child to develop a love for reading. Readers are the only people who truly remain educated.

6. Do not treat your children as failures for lack of academic performance or heroes for their academic success. Try to help them and encourage them but do not offer predictions on their chances for future success based on their school performance.

7. Avoid trying to live your child's life. If allowed to uncover their purpose in life he will excel beyond even the grandest hopes you have for him.

8. Try to encourage your child to go to college but do make the decision for them. If it appears that college does not seem to be in your child's future then try to encourage them to learn about successful people who do not have college educations. There are several examples to choose from including Michael

Dell, Sir Richard Branson of the Virgin Records/Airlines, and the non-college educated individuals on the Forbes Wealthiest List noted above. The child may never have the success of these individuals but it will show him that there can be success without college and provide a role model on how to achieve that success.

Believers & Doubters

Meet Some of the Non-gifted

1. **Einstein** was four years old before he could speak and seven before he could read.

2. **Isaac Newton** did poorly in grade school.

3. When **Thomas Edison** was a boy, his teachers told his mother he was too stupid to learn anything.

4. A newspaper editor fired **Walt Disney** because he had "No good ideas"

5. **Enrico Caruso's** music teacher told him "You can't sing, you have no voice at all." (Caruso was a famous tenor, like Pavaroti is today.)

6. **Leo Tolstoy** flunked out of college.

7. **Werner Von Braun** flunked 9th grade algebra.

8. **Louis Pasteur** was rated as mediocre in chemistry when he attended the Royal College

9. **Abraham Lincoln** entered The Black Hawk War as a captain and came out a private

10. **Winston Churchill** failed the sixth grade.

Myth #3
Helping kids gives them an advantage or head start in life

In his book Dr Stanley has discovered that the more parents help their children the less successful the children are in life. In reality, by not helping your child you are providing him an opportunity to build confidence that many good intentioned parents fail to take advantage of. You are doing more for your child by encouraging them to do for him or herself than you doing it for them. Even the most cherished of parents' goals, paying for college, can actually be harmful to your child. Studies have shown that those who pay for their own education are more likely to have successful lives than those whose parents put them through school. The basic reason for this is that those who are paying for their education see that it is worth the sacrifice while those who are going to school "on someone else's dime" usually see it as an extension of their high school years. You are actually doing more for your child by providing enthusiastic support than financial support.

A few years ago I was at a conference where a police officer was giving a lecture on youth crime. While giving his speech he touched on family values and mentioned that you will not see what your family values are until your children are 35 and have a family of their own. How they treat their family is a reflection of how you treated yours. This is the main reason that raising children is the hardest endeavor we can take. Since we may not see the results of our efforts for at least a couple of decades it is difficult to know if what we are doing to a child is correct or incorrect, healthy or harmful. For most of us it is an act of faith that we are doing our best and our best is good enough. This is further compounded by the fact that in order to teach them what is correct parents often must go against society and even the "knowledgeable" experts. In many cases they feel like a salmon trying to swim upstream and may wonder if they are really making an impact. They often ask themselves if the lessons are being learned or are they just wasting their time? In fact at times it may even feel as if there is a constant battle being waged for their child's heart and mind. The fact is that there is a battle being waged and we must fight for our children's hearts and minds. In this battle it is essential that we avoid being the paternalistic dictator who controls rather than encourages. You will do better to work with your child by helping him discover his own purpose in life and to teach him to be a Believer.

Myth #4
Children need to be socialized at a young age

I believe this to be the most dangerous of all myths. Every parent knows the danger of peer pressure. That in a very short amount of time it can undo all that the parent has taught the child. It can lead the child to drug and alcohol abuse, a promiscuous lifestyle, or a gang member's life of crime. It is what parents fear the most for it is the greatest threat that faces our children.

Yet, it is the one danger in which parents do all they can to insure that their children fall victim to it. Early socialization of children, via daycare and preschool, exposes them to group situations before their own identities have had the chance to be developed. They learn at a very young and impressionable age to conform to the standards and norms of their peers. This dangerous combination almost ensures that they will develop the habit of "crowd pleasing" and thus be at the mercy of each peer group they encounter. This greatly reduces their chances to resist the negative lifestyles that permeate today's youth culture.

I am not saying pre-school is bad or that daycare needs to be avoided. What I am saying is that these need to be moderated and balanced with the child having an equal amount of alone time. As Riesman points out, these times are essential to the child's development since it is during these periods of solitude that a child discovers his own identity. He becomes aware of himself and discovers who he is. It is where he develops his own likes and dislikes, thoughts and opinions, and becomes aware of his talents and abilities. This self-awareness is what makes him become a self-reliant, purposeful, independent thinking individual who can resist the pressure of the group. It also increases the child's chances of being a leader rather than a follower.

So do not be in a hurry to socialize your child and do not worry if he wants some alone time. It is a normal and healthy part of development. It will not make him anti-social nor will he end up someday in a bell tower with a high-power rifle. You will be allowing him to learn the pleasure of just being himself.

On a final note, you are the parent. Parents know their children like no one else. Parents, especially mothers, instinctively know what is right for their children. Have faith in your instincts, your intuition, and your abilities to raise your child. Children are not as fragile as the experts would like us to believe. If they were then the human race would have never made it out of the caves. Also recall that experts are a product of the society they grew up in and the advice they give often reflects that mindset. In today's society that means it is probably the advice of the Other-directed personality and the mindset of a Doubter.

CHAPTER FOURTEEN
Back to the Basics

Life is not easy for any of us. But what of that? We must have perseverance and, above all, confidence in ourselves. We must believe that we are gifted for something and that this thing must be attained.
- Marie Curie (1867-1934)

A common assumption that people make when they are introduced to principles and philosophies that they are unfamiliar with is to believe that it is novel, new, or unique. Maybe even a mark of a genius. This is what I did as my dad shared his wisdom and knowledge with me. After all it was not what society as a whole was learning and so I assumed that it was something unique to my dad. But as I became older and started to learn things on my own I came to realize that the principles that created my dad's attitude about life were not his principles. They were the principles of his time.

I came rather late into the lives of my parents. At age 36 my dad was ten years older than the fathers of most newborns. This and fact that my dad, after the death of his father, started dealing with adult issues at the age of eight meant that he came into adulthood in the late 1930s. So while most of the parents of my peers were still in grade school my dad was servicing Navy aircraft on a Pacific island while avoiding being shot by Japanese soldiers.

As a result my dad became a product of a time when existence was not guaranteed. A time when there wasn't any welfare, especially in depression ravaged rural Alabama, and social security was still just an untried concept. A time when no one was entitled to anything, it all had to be earned. A time when people did not give you a job, a paycheck, or anything else- you were expected to provide for yourself. A time that saw a depression wipeout savings and leave those who put their faith in money lost, destitute, and without hope. A time when one's ability to earn money meant the difference between a full and empty stomach, being warm or cold, and being wet or dry. A time that required one to have faith in oneself or suffer the fate of the weak willed.

A time when America's inner-directed society produced men and women who survived the depression and went on to sacrifice more than 400,000 of its sons, husbands, daughters and wives to defeat the tyranny of fascism. Men and women who understood that being a responsible individual meant acting and thinking for oneself with each person having the right to claim the glory of their successes while suffering the agonies of their failures. Men and women to whom freedom to dream and build, to succeed and fail was prized more than security. Although they worked to earn a living they would be appalled by the idea of being a kept person whose livelihood was dependent on the generosity of their employer or government beneficence. Their dignity was more important than any handout that may begotten by cowing to a master and thus making them what Tom Brokaw would call the "Greatest Generation."

If you ask my mom she would tell you they were not great. It was the attitude and principles they had to have to survive. It was what had to be done and it was what was expected just like her six brothers going off to fight the Japanese and her other brother escaping that war only to be sent to fight in Korea. It was also a time when they took pride in who and what they were and, although there weren't any safety nets like welfare and social security, they did not feel insecure because they knew they had what it took to survive the greatest financial crisis in history and the most destructive war the world has ever seen.

Of course these principles and attitudes are not unique to the "Greatest Generation." They have been key to the development of all the great freedom loving and democratic civilizations since the Greeks. They can be found in the earliest days of the Romans only disappear during the servitude years of the Dark Ages. They then reappeared to ignite an era of discovery and enlightenment that started with the Renaissance and continues to this day. This is why I have inserted quotes from the greatest thinkers, statesmen, philosophers, and commercialists that these societies have produced. They re-enforce that the principles I lay down on these pages are not unique, nor new, nor novel. They are just forgotten.

The main question becomes, "If these principles were so instrumental in the rise of western civilization why were they forgotten?" The answer to that is what economists know as the law of unintended consequences. This law states that actions of people—and especially of government—always have effects that are unanticipated or unintended. The combination of the economic turmoil of the 1930's and the unparalleled economic prosperity that followed, as America became the "Arsenal of Democracy" in the 1940s, created two different conditions that had similar unintended consequences.

The first was President Roosevelt's New Deal plan. This plan created programs and agencies that would help rescue America from the clutches of the depression that was sweeping the world. One of the ways it attempted to do this was by providing a safety net that would offer temporary protection for Americans suffering financial hardships. It was very controversial at the time as aspects of it were thought to be socialistic and several of its more extreme parts were struck down by the Supreme Court. The effectiveness of this plan is still being debated but it should be remembered that most of the programs that made up the plan were intended to provide short-term relief. In fact almost all if its programs were dissolved or abandoned with the onset of the World War because it was believed that Americans, in prosperity, would return to their self-reliant, productive, and enterprising ways.

This was followed in the 1940s by what was the starting point of unequaled growth and prosperity for American corporations. The worldwide demand for war material and the fact that the United States was the sole industrialized country that did not have a war raging on its land meant that the United States became the biggest supplier of materials for the allied armies. American weapons, vehicles, and material helped keep the armies of the British Empire, France, China and the Soviet Union supplied and on the field of battle. The end of the war found the industrial capacity of all the other combatant nations severely damaged, if not destroyed, and it would once again be American corporations, via the Marshal Plan, that would be instrumental in the reconstruction of the devastated nations of the world. An economy based on large corporations employing a large percentage of the workforce appeared to be the way of the future and it looked as if corporatism was here to stay.

As prosperity continued to grow workers became the beneficiaries of corporate largess and within thirty years

70% of them were employees of large corporations. In order to compete for skilled labor corporations had to take steps to attract and keep employees. This led not only to an increase in wages but also to what became to be known as "fringe benefits". These additional enticements required employers to take over some of the responsibility that the workers were historically responsible for. This included the health needs of their families and the provision of providing for the employees' livelihood when they are older and no longer able or willing to work.

Soon 'fringe benefits" and other incentives such as seniority and increased income based solely on the time one has been with the company were considered just as important as the wages one earned. This would often bind an employee to the company and created an expectation of lifetime employment. Job security became a principle and was the utmost important goal for most workers. There appeared to many an implied promise that if a worker gave 30 or 40 years to a company then that company had the responsibility to take care of them. Cradle to grave employment and benefits were expected.

Another consequence of the dominance of corporations was that business, government, and the professions became "heavily bureaucratized." This is why David Riesman did not see being an "Other-directed" personality as a negative when he published *The Lonely Crowd* in 1950. Their desire for approval and their ability to conform allowed them to thrive in the new corporate driven economy. As Riesman explains, this caused a shift in the dominating character of the United States and being an educated self-thinker became second to being a compliant controllable corporate employee. This was the unintended consequence of these two events. Unlike what FDR thought the American character did not return to the pre-New Deal principles that had made the country great. Instead it became "other-directed" with people being wholly dependent on the government and corporate generosity

As any good parent knows the more they do for their child the less that child does for himself. This is human nature and it does not end with the coming of age or maturity. The more that the government did for its citizens and corporations did for their workers the less the people did for themselves. Unlike the self-reliant Americans of the previous 200 years, people came to rely on the others for their survival. Unfortunately for those born during this time, such as the Baby Boomers, they have no understanding of it being any different. This is the danger that Dr. Hayak warned us about in *The Road to Serfdom* (1944). He saw that the real threat the ideals of socialism and the welfare state has on a society is not financial but psychological. That within a generation or two the people of that society go from being independent and self-reliant to being dependent with the need to look to others to provide solutions to their problems. They begin to believe they are entitled to certain things and look for someone to "give" them a job with a livable wage no matter what their skill level is. They start to see politicians and others as saviors whose primary responsibility is to look after the people's welfare. What is worse is that these politicians see themselves in the same role and government takes on a paternalistic approach. There is no better example of this than the man who, in a town hall meeting, asked President Clinton, "We are your children. What are you going to do for us?"

These are the attitudes that set my parents apart from those of my peers. For many of my friends their parents came of age in the late 1950s/early 1960s and were the products of an Other-directed society. To them the only way to have "meaning" in life is to concentrate on people, relationships, and feelings. The attitudes of my parents' generation were condemned as being cold and heartless. By focusing on results rather than intentions and individuality rather than collectivism Inner-directed people were seen to be lacking compassion.

The problem is that Believers have a different understanding of what "meaning" and compassion is. They know that it is by focusing on results and individualism that they make their lives "meaningful" and compassionate. They are driven by a sense of duty to use their abilities for the maximization of human potential and that they must contribute to people's lives in a productive way. They also understand that this focus on one's duty to live up to his full potential is the only way to ensure that they live the best life they are capable of while maintaining their freedom and independence. They understand that true security comes not from the government or employer but from within oneself. They also understand that the more a person or entity is responsible for someone the less control that person has over himself. This loss of freedom is more than they are willing to pay.

What Riesman could not predict in 1950 was the role that technology would play in bringing about the end of corporate dominance. He could not foresee how the development of the personal computer and the internet would give birth to the Information/Digital age. An age when that would allow less than a dozen employees to do the work that once required a hundred. These changes saw a rise of cottage industries that were comprised of small businesses. A new age of entrepreneurial-ism, which offered endless opportunities, was ushered in. This has allowed small and medium sized businesses to replace the large corporation as America's principle employers. It also created an environment that demanded more of the employees.

Additionally, unlike David Riesman, my dad did not believe that the large corporation was here to stay. He understood that it was impossible to maintain the government and corporate paternalism that many had come to expect. That the financial situation that had existed since 1940 was an anomaly that is only possible during the most ideal situations. The death of the corporate pension plans, the current fight over healthcare benefits, and the pending collapse of the Social Security system all appear to be proving him correct. Furthermore, it has taken me eighteen months to write this book and during that time almost 5,000,000 Americans have lost their jobs, the financial markets are in a meltdown, and an ever worsening economic situation threatens to lead us into another depression.

Whether this does come to pass or not the two previously discussed changes means that life for the Doubter has become a lot more difficult. With the end of corporate dominance it is no longer sufficient to be an Other-directed personality that dutifully performs his assigned tasks and who gets along well with others. With almost 90% of all new jobs being created by small companies today's employee will be required, with little or no supervision, to perform multiple task, handle multiple responsibilities, and to contribute to the decision- making process. In essence he will need to have the mindset of a Believer. This means a return to the basic attitudes and philosophies of my parents' generation.

Changing a lifetime of training is not easy and as a country we are still looking to others to save us. During all this economic turmoil we had an historical election that resulted in the first black president being elected. Many voted with the hope that he will save them. That somehow President Obama will change not only our country but also their situations. I hope he can but I am not holding my breath. Not because of who he is but because of who I am. I know that the only person who has the power to change my life is me and that my success, security, and prosperity does not come from the government or employer or anyone else. It comes from within and those who recognize and tap into it become autonomous individuals who control their destiny regardless of who the president is. This is what I was taught to believe and the same can go for you.

I am not going to kid you. Life is hard. In fact life is so hard that you will not get out of it alive. It is a roller coaster with ups and downs, good times and bad times, happiness and sadness, rejoicing and sorrow. This is true of everyone's lives and as I have illustrated in this book there is no avoiding its peeks and valleys. Life does not give you the option to ride the merry-go-round. No matter how much you wish it to be otherwise, you are on the roller coaster. By ignoring this you end up riding an ostrich with its head in the ground instead of a determined stallion. As Helen Keller highlights no matter how safe you try to be you can still be caught unaware or in danger.

> Life is not easy for any of us. But what of that?
> -Marie Curie

We can also learn from Henry Ford's warning to put faith not in money but in ourselves. This is the objective of this book: to help you start developing faith in yourself. Firstly, education does not stop with a degree or a good career. It is a lifelong task that needs to be pursued with all the fervor one can muster. Just like food nourishes the body education nourishes the mind. A starved mind is not any good to anyone. Like any other body part, it starts dying if not used. Secondly, do not be afraid to falter and fail because it will happen. Only by trying can you succeed and the most important thing is not that you failed but what you do afterwards. Get up and move on. I know you can do it because you have already done it when you were a baby. You fell and fell but now you walk! Amazing what we can do when we do not yet have the fears of adulthood holding us back!

While I have shared with you a lifetime of learning in these pages I urge you not to blindly accept me or anyone else who claims to be an expert on any subject. I beg you to strike out on your own journey of knowledge and understanding. It can be a very fulfilling and liberating experience. This is why I have covered various topics like culture and religion. For many these are considered taboo subjects. It is not my desire to change your views or convert you. I did this to give you a starting point from which you can begin thinking for yourself. To question some of what you may unquestioningly take as fact including conventional wisdom, expert advise, religious teachings and cultural conditioning. To understand that these may not be, and in many cases were not, designed for the benefit of the individual person. It is important to remember and accept that all cultures and religions have good and bad aspects. I do not think there is an example of either one that has not been tainted by man's desire to dominate and control others. Even if you believe the Bible is the word of God you must accept that man's selective use of the gospel serve's his purposes not His. If you doubt this then I urge you to ask yourself, "Why do we say 'money is the root of all evil' and not the complete verse which states 'the love of money is the root of all evil'?" Read chapter 3 if you are not sure.

In any religion, culture, society, country, and family there are aspects that that rightly deserve criticism. I do not agree with those who believe that blind faith, obedience, and resistance to differing opinions are how you show respect. On the contrary, you show respect by being the best example of the religion, culture, society, country, and family that you can be even if it means rejecting some of its harmful teachings and beliefs. I believe that as citizens of the United States and as members of the human race we have a duty to think for ourselves, to question those who wish to think for us. No matter who they are. Remember, Hitler was a political leader and Jim Jones was a pastor. Those who blindly followed them met their doom. In Hitler's case many innocent lives were lost with the final death toll being about 40 million. This was only possible because so many people lacking faith in themselves refused to use the brain that God or nature gave them.

Even though I intended for this book to focus on the differences between Believers and Doubters and how those mindsets affect how we live, I did dedicate a lot of words to money. This is for three reasons. The first is as a financial advisor and tax preparer this is the area of people's lives in which I have had a lot of access to and am able to see how people relate to it. The second is that it is an area where one can clearly see how the mindsets help or hurts one's effort in life. The final reason is that money, while not the most important, is a very important part of our lives. It determines our lifestyle, health, education, and the ability to care for ourselves and those we love. In fact money is important to all of us.

An example of this is a discussion I had with a woman who told me money was not important to her. She said she grew up never having it so she never felt the need to try and get it now. I asked her to imagine that she was holding $500. "Now," I said, "what would you say if I told you that there was an investment that would guarantee you $100,000 in three months if you invested that five hundred today. No possible way of losing, insured, guaranteed. What would you do?"

"I would give the $500," she said.

"Why," I asked.

"Because I am not going to walk away from $100,000," she replied.

"But what if it was not guaranteed?" I went on, "What if there was a chance of losing the $500. Would you still invest the $500?"

"No," she said, "money is not that important to me."

"No, money is important to you," I replied. "You just said so when you said that you would not walk away from it. In fact it is so important that you are scared to lose it. That is why you do not have it. It is too important to you."

Lastly, while this may be the end of the book I hope that it is the beginning for you. A beginning that gives you the knowledge and power to see things differently and to question some of the beliefs, philosophies, thoughts, and attitudes you have. A beginning that allows you to develop personally. A beginning that allows you to identify areas in your life where your mindset maybe holding you down instead of lifting you up. A beginning that allows you to discover alternative and more productive ways of thinking. A beginning that starts your life as a Believer and ends the limited life of a Doubter. Yes life is hard, but that does not mean that we have to stop living it.

"Our deepest fear is not that we are inadequate. Our deepest fear is that we are powerful beyond measure. It is our light, not our darkness that most frightens us. We ask ourselves, Who am I to be brilliant, gorgeous, talented, fabulous? Actually, who are you *not* to be? You are a child of God. Your playing small does not serve the world. There is nothing enlightened about shrinking so that other people won't feel insecure around you. We are all meant to shine, as children do. We were born to make manifest the glory of God that is within us. It's not just in some of us; it's in everyone. And as we let our own light shine, we unconsciously give other people permission to do the same. As we are liberated from our own fear, our presence automatically liberates others."

- Marianne Williamson
from *A Return To Love: Reflections on the Principles of A Course in Miracles*

APPENDIX I
Additional Knowledge

Books

Walter Russell Mead,
God & Gold: Britain, America and the Making of the Modern World, Knopf Publishing. (Chapters 2 and 3 deal with how culture and religion can help or hamper prosperity)

Dr. Thomas J. Stanley Ph.D.
The Millionaire Next Door, Andrew McNeel Publishing
The Millionaire Mind, Andrew McNeel Publishing
(Two academic but very enlightening books that break many misconceptions society has about millionaires and wealth)

Robert Kiyosaki
Rich Dad/Poor Dad, Warner Business Books
Retire Young/Retire Rich, Warner Business Books
(If read in the order listed these are natural follow ups to this book)

Donald Trump and Robert Kiyosaki
Why We Want You to be Rich, Rich Press
(An excellent book that highlights why society needs the successful and prosperous individuals who create wealth for all of the others)

T. Harv Eker
Secrets of the Millionaire Mindset, Harper Business Books
(A book that uses the compare and contrast method to illustrate the differences in the way successful and non-successful people think)

While there are hundreds of books in the personal achievement genre I find the above to be the best ones to start your journey with. Being mindset focused they will help you to develop the attitude needed to be a Believer.

Appendix I

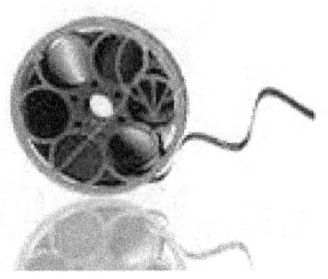

Movies

I highly recommend these two movies. They provide visual contrasts between individuals from Open and Closed societies. Additionally they are both great family films.

Goal: The Dream Begins (2005) Milkshake Films

Bend it Like Beckham (2002), Kintop Pictures

Last Holiday (2006) Paramount Pictures
(This is an excellent movie that illustrates what can happen when we give up the Fear of Living)

CDs/Audio

These are some programs that I have listened to and have found very enlightening. Nightingale-Conant is the leader of such products and I suggest that you visit their website at www.nightingale.com for a more details.

Earl Nightingale
Lead the Field
The Strangest Secret

Napoleon Hill
The Science of Personal Achievement

Brian Tracy
The Psychology of Achievement

Appendix II

STAYING INFORMED

Website

www.libertylanemedia.com

- New Products
- Event Info
- Sneek Pre-views of future books

E-Mail

believers@libertylanemedia.com

- Submit comments and questions
- Request John to speak to your group or organization
- Share your story

Blog

www.believersanddoubters.wordpress.com

- Timely and relevant topics
- Read the thoughts and opitions of others
- Share your thoughts and opinions

Believers & Doubters

  Since 1994 John Hancock has assisted hundreds of people with their financial needs and goals. This relationship has provided him with a look into people's lives that very few ever get. It goes beyond the image building and gets right to the heart of their situations. Through these unique experiences he has been able to observe how people behave in good as well as difficult times. Additionally, John's BA degree in International Business gave him an understanding of how culture, traditions, and religious beliefs affect the attitudes that determined people's view of themselves and the world in which they live in.

  It was not long after John started to share this knowledge with others that he was asked to speak at various events including workshops for business, professional, educational, and religious organizations. Seeing that his audiences wanted more in early 2008 John started working on *Believers & Doubters.* His writing generated great interest and the highlight of his efforts came in the summer of 2008 when he recognized in a press release by Donald Trump's Trump University and was asked to be a guest-presenter for their students. John was further honored by Trump University when in October of 2008 he was selected to be interviewed for a video that is played on their website and at their seminars nationwide.

Notes

www.ingramcontent.com/pod-product-compliance
Lightning Source LLC
Chambersburg PA
CBHW031346040426
42444CB00005B/211